# SCHOTT'S
# FOOD & DRINK
# MISCELLANY

# SCHOTT'S
# FOOD & DRINK
# MISCELLANY

*Conceived, written, and designed by*

## BEN SCHOTT

BLOOMSBURY

Schott's Food & Drink Miscellany™

© BEN SCHOTT 2003

Published by Bloomsbury Publishing Plc.
38 Soho Square, London, W1D 3HB, UK

www.miscellanies.info

10  9  8  7  6  5  4  3  2  1

The above numbers (sometimes referred to as 'reprint' or 'strikeout' numbers)
provide information on the print-run of a book: the lowest number visible
shows the run from which the book originated.

Cover illustration © Alison Lang 2003
The illustrations on pp.42, 54, 92, 96–7, 120, 142 © Chris Lyon 2003
Other illustrations © Ben Schott 2003

The author cannot accept responsibility for any medical, nutritional,
or food-safety issues. If in any doubt seek expert advice.

ISBN 0-7475-6654-2
A CIP catalogue record for this book is available from the British Library.

Designed and typeset by BEN SCHOTT
Printed in Great Britain by CLAYS Ltd, ST IVES Plc.

# SCHOTT'S
# FOOD & DRINK
# MISCELLANY

An olla podrida? A smorgasbord? A hot pot? An ambigu?
A salmagundi? An amphigouri? A cocktail? A bouquet garni?
A rumfustian? A mirepoix? A kickshaw? A flummery?

*Schott's Food & Drink Miscellany* is all of these and, perhaps, more.

*Schott's Food & Drink Miscellany* is a snapper-up of unconsidered trifles
(in both senses of the word, see p.20). The book's purpose is to sweep up
the crumbs strewn carelessly across the conversational table-cloth.

*Schott's Food & Drink Miscellany* makes very few claims to be exhaustive,
authoritative, or even practical. In a kitchen the size of the *Miscellany* one
could never attempt to prepare a full *à la carte* service – instead, the book
hopes to whet the appetite with a gourmet tasting menu, or *dégustation*.

---
## THE FOUNDATION OF TRUTH
---

Painstaking efforts have been made to ensure that all of the information
contained within the *Miscellany* is accurate. However, the author cannot
accept responsibility if you order a dish that doesn't agree with you; drink
out of turn from the Loving Cup; say something inappropriate during
grace; cook an inordinate quantity of spaghetti; or poison your favourite
aunt. As Carl Jung said: 'Mistakes are, after all, the foundations of truth.'

Any suggestions[†], corrections, clarifications, cocktails, or recipes may be
emailed to food@miscellanies.info – or sent by post to the author care of
Bloomsbury Publishing Plc., 38 Soho Square, London, W1D 3HB, UK.

> [*Menu spellings are often curious and rarely consistent. Original spellings
> are quoted verbatim, no matter how odd they seem. Readers of* Schott's
> Original Miscellany *may notice a few minor duplications. It was
> decided that to omit these might detract from the present book. Wherever
> possible these entries have been elaborated and expanded upon.*]

[†]The author reserves the right to treat all suggestions and recipes as his own, and to
employ them in future editions, other endeavours, or just to add piquancy to his cooking.

I am indebted to the following people who have been more than generous with their support, advice, encouragement, expertise, and experience:

Jonathan, Judith, and Geoffrey Schott.

Clare Algar, Stephen Aucutt, Bill Baker, Joanna Begent,
Clare Bernard, Martin Birchall, Lisa Birdwood, John Casey,
James Coleman, Martin Colyer, Victoria Cook, Aster Crawshaw,
Rosemary Davidson, Jody Davies, Liz Davies, Mary Davis,
Jennifer Epworth, James Fitzsimons, Penny Gillinson, Kate Gunning,
Gaynor Hall, Charlotte Hawse, Highgate Bookshop, Max Jones,
Hugo de Klee, Yuko Komiyama-Folan, Alison Lang, Rachel Law,
John Lloyd, David Loewi, Ruth Logan, Chris Lyon, Jess Manson,
Michael Manson, Susannah McFarlane, Colin Midson,
Charles Miller, David Miller, Sarah Myerscough, Polly Napper,
Sandy Nelson, Sarah Norton, Oonagh Phelan, Cally Poplak,
Dave Powell, Daniel Rosenthal, Tom Rosenthal, Sarah Sands,
Carolyne Sibley, Rachel Simhon, Caroline Sullivan,
Nicky Thompson, David Ward, Ann Warnford-Davis,
William Webb, and Caitlin Withey.

Restaurants and bars favoured by the above named may be seen on p.152.

First, catch your hare…


— HANNAH GLASSE[†]


---

[†]Sadly, it seems that this much-loved quotation is, in fact, a misquotation. The recipe of English cook Hannah Glasse actually starts with the instruction: '*Take your hare when it is cas'd and make a Pudding*' – *cas'd* here meaning skinned. Hannah Glasse (1708–70) was habit-maker to the Prince of Wales, and author of a number of popular texts, including one of the first cookbooks in England – *The Art of Cookery made Plain and Easy* (1747).

## EQUINE SAVOURIES

| ANGELS ON HORSEBACK | DEVILS ON HORSEBACK |
|---|---|
| Oysters wrapped in streaky bacon, grilled & served on buttered toast. | Prunes wrapped in streaky bacon, grilled & served on buttered toast. |

## SAFFRON

Saffron is extracted from an autumn-flowering, lilac-flowered species of crocus *(Crocus sativus)*, a member of the Iridaceae family. Its name derives from the Arabic *za'fran* ('be yellow'). What is commonly referred to as saffron is, in fact, the thin, branching stigmas of this crocus; each cultivated saffron crocus has three stigmas that are plucked by hand. Up to 150,000 flowers are required to produce one kilogram of dried saffron. It is this ratio that has secured saffron's status as one of the most expensive of all spices, often worth more than its weight in gold. Saffron is intensely fragrant, although occasionally bitter, and is commonly employed as a seasoning or colourant. (To obtain the colour from dried saffron one should soak the strands in water for some hours.) Perhaps because of its scarcity and price saffron has long been considered an aphrodisiac. It is said that Zeus slept upon a bed of saffron; marriage veils in many cultures used to be dyed with saffron (or were coloured yellow); and wealthy Romans would scatter crocus stigmas upon their marriage beds – which might help to explain the latin tag referring to light-hearted exhilaration:

> *dormvit in sacco croci* — he has slept in a bed of saffron

## FORMAL MEAL TIMES

C19th servants were expected to serve meals according to these rules:

| Announced time | Actual time |
|---|---|
| 6 o'clock | 7 o'clock |
| 6 o'clock precisely | 6·30 o'clock |
| No later than 6 o'clock | 6 o'clock |

## SMOKE-RINGS

Blowing smoke-rings is easier done than said. One technique is to take a mouthful of smoke, push the tongue flat against the mouth's floor, form one's lips into a circle (as if one were saying 'oh!') and push the smoke through one's lips, not by blowing, but by contracting the gullet in pulses.

## POPCORN: HISTORY & ORDERING

Popcorn is made by roasting dried kernels of maize *(Zea mays everta)* with fat. As the maize heats, the starch inside swells and bursts forth from the kernel's outer skin. Popcorn's early use has been traced across South America, and it seems that popping maize kernels was a key element in some of the ceremonies of C16th Aztec Indians. Only in 1893 did Charles C. Cretors develop the world's first mobile popcorn machine, making the bulk manufacture of the snack a reality. Ordering popcorn at the cinema presents a dilemma. Sweet popcorn alone can become sickly, and salted popcorn alone can cause unwelcome dehydration. The ideal solution, therefore, is to order both kinds.

Research suggests that the best method is to have the lower half of the carton filled with sweet popcorn, with salted popcorn filling the remaining space *(see diagram opposite)*. Thus, just at the point when the salinity becomes overwhelming, the sweet layer is discovered, offering variety and respite.

*salted*

*sweet*

## GOURMANDS & INDIGESTION

According to the legendary French food writer and critic, Grimod de la Reynière (1690–1756): 'The true gourmand never ventures out without an emetic; it is the quickest and safest way to avoid the effects of indigestion.'

## MELBA TOAST

It is said that Melba toast was created especially for the opera singer Nellie Melba – the stage-name of Helen Porter Mitchell (1861–1931). Auguste Escoffier, the chef at César Ritz's famous hotel, is thought to have devised the snack to ameliorate Dame Melba's diet during her illness in 1897; César Ritz is credited with naming it. It is perfectly possible that all this is true, but the simplicity of making Melba toast (indeed the likelihood of making it, or something similar, by accident) suggests that Escoffier and Ritz did little more than name an existing technique. Most shop-bought Melba toast is execrable, but making it is utterly straightforward:

*Lightly toast slices of bread and, while they are still warm,*
*slice them through their middles into two thin halves.*
*Re-toast the halves (a warm oven is ideal) until the edges start to curl.*

Melba toast is an ideal accompaniment to pâté, cheese, and thin soups.

# THE MONSTER EGG

The 'monster egg' is a curious exhibition recipe sadly long out of fashion:

> *Break a dozen or two of eggs and separate the whites from the yolks. Tie the yolks in a pig's bladder, boil them hard, and remove them. In a larger pig's bladder, place the whites. Into the midst of the whites, place the set yolks and tie the bladder tight. Boil the whole until the whites harden and then remove from the water. Serve the Monster Egg on a bed of spinach.*

# CHEERS! AROUND THE WORLD

| | | | |
|---|---|---|---|
| Afrikaans | Gesondheid! | Italian | Salute! |
| Albanian | Gëzuar! | Japanese | *kampai!* |
| Amharic | Desta! | Latin | Bibite! |
| Breton | Yehed mad! | Maori | Kia ora! |
| Catalan | Salut! | Morse code | —·— ··· ·· ··· |
| Chinese | *ganbei!* | Norwegian | Skål! |
| Danish | Skål! | Pig Latin | Eerschay! |
| Dutch | Proost! | Polish | Na zdrowie! |
| Esperanto | Je via sano! | Portuguese | Saúde! |
| Finnish | Kippis! | Romanian | Noroc! |
| French | A votre santé! | Russian | *na zdorovye!* |
| Gaelic (Irish) | Sláinte! | Serbocroatian | Ziveli! |
| German | Prost! | Spanish | ¡Salud! |
| Greek | *ebiba!* | Swahili | Hongera! |
| Greek (ancient) | *hygeia!* | Taiwanese | *hotala!* |
| Hebrew | L'chaim! | Welsh | Iechyd da! |

# HYSTERON PROTERON

The 'Hysteron Proteron' was a dining club at Balliol College, Oxford, described by the writer Evelyn Waugh in his glorious autobiography *A Little Learning*: '… members put themselves to great discomfort by living a day in reverse, getting up in evening dress, drinking whiskey, smoking cigars and playing cards, then at ten o'clock dining backwards starting with savouries and ending with soup.' The term hysteron proteron derives from the Greek *hysteros* – 'later', and *protos* – 'first'. It is more commonly employed to describe the rhetorical technique where the normal order of a phrase is reversed for dramatic or ironic effect. An oft-quoted example of hysteron proteron is taken from Virgil: *moriamur et in media arma ruamus* – 'let us die and charge into the thick of the fight' [*Aeneid* ii. 358].

## CURDS & WHEY

Curd is the solid that separates from coagulated milk, whey is the liquid.

Little Miss Muffet
Sat on a tuffet,
Eating some curds and whey.
Along came a spider,
And sat down beside her,
And frightened Miss Muffet away.

TRADITIONAL NURSERY RHYME

I'll make you feed on berries
and on roots, And feed on curds
and whey, and suck the goat,
And cabin in a cave, and bring
you up To be a warrior, and
command a camp.

TITUS ANDRONICUS IV.ii

## CIGAR COLOUR NOMENCLATURE

Cigar factories in Cuba would commonly distinguish between two hundred shades of tobacco. Nowadays, around sixty terms are employed – though these can be simplified to seven basic colours, listed here in order of lightness:

*clarissimo – green*
*claro claro – blonde*
*claro – café au lait*
*colorado claro – light-brown*
*maduro colorado – reddish-brown*
*maduro – dark brown*
*oscuro – black*

## MACARONI

The tubes of pasta known as macaroni (see p.96) were probably introduced into English cuisine by a group of young, rich, well-travelled dandies who slavishly aped Continental style and custom – in Horace Walpole's words 'travelled young men who wear long curls and spying-glasses'. They formed the Macaroni Club, which dined in ostentatious style at Almack's club. In 1770 the *Oxford Magazine* described these insolent fops thus:

*There is indeed a kind of animal, neither male nor female, a thing of the neuter gender, lately started up amongst us. It is called a Macaroni. It talks without meaning, it smiles without pleasantry, it eats without appetite, it rides without exercise, it wenches without passion.*

## BLOOD ALCOHOL CONTENT LIMIT

The maximum quantity of alcohol that drivers in Britain are permitted to have in their bloodstream is 80mg of alcohol per 100ml of blood. (50mg in France, Austria, Denmark, and Germany; 20mg in Sweden.)

## ENGLISH TO AMERICAN FOOD TERMS

| English | American |
|---|---|
| Aubergine | eggplant |
| Bain marie | double boiler |
| Banger | sausage |
| Bap | hamburger bun |
| Boiled sweet | hard candy |
| Broad bean | fava/lima bean |
| Candy floss | cotton candy |
| Caster sugar | superfine sugar |
| Chicory | endive |
| Chips | French or Freedom fries |
| Clingfilm | plastic wrap |
| Conserves | preserves |
| Coriander | cilantro |
| Cornflour | cornstarch |
| Courgette | zucchini |
| Crisps | potato chips |
| Cutlet | chop |
| Cream, double | heavy cream |
| Cream, single | light cream |
| Faggot | meatball |
| Fairy cake | cup cake |
| Fish fingers | fish sticks |
| French beans | string beans |
| Frying pan | skillet |
| Gammon | ham |
| Glacé fruits | candied fruits |
| Greaseproof paper | wax paper |
| Green/red pepper | bell pepper |
| Grill (verb) | broil |
| Hundreds & thousands | sprinkles |
| Hull (verb) | shuck |
| Ice lolly | popsicle |
| Icing | frosting |
| Icing sugar | confectioner's sugar |
| Jacket potato | baked potato |
| Jam | jelly |
| Jelly | jello |
| Kipper | smoked herring |
| Liquidizer | blender |
| Mangetout | snow peas |
| Mince | ground meat |
| Muesli | granola |
| Muslin | cheesecloth |
| Offal (see p.70) | variety meats |
| Pasty† | meat wrap |
| Paw paw | papaya |
| Plonk | cheap wine |
| Porridge | oatmeal |
| Prawn | shrimp |
| Profiterole | cream puff |
| Pudding | dessert |
| Semolina | cream of wheat |
| Shandy | beer and lemonade |
| Sirloin (steak) | porterhouse |
| Snifter | cocktail |
| Sorbet | sherbert |
| Spring onions | scallions |
| Squash (drink) | juice |
| Starter | appetizer |
| Stock cube | bouillon cube |
| Sultanas | golden raisins |
| Swede | rutabaga |
| Sweet | dessert |
| Tin foil | aluminum wrap |
| Tinned | canned |
| Toffee | taffy |
| Treacle | molasses |

†The word 'pasty' should be used with care in the United States. In England, pasties are semi-circular pastries with savoury fillings, traditional in Devon and Cornwall. In America, however, pasties are the nipple-tassels worn by strippers.

## DORMICE

The Romans developed a taste for the edible dormouse *(Myoxus glis)*, which they fattened in special cages *(gliraria)* before stuffing and roasting.

## COFFEE AND BREWER

According to Ebenezer Cobham Brewer (although no other source has been forthcoming) ten cups of coffee used to be drunk after dinner in the Ardennes, each with a special name and an increasingly alcoholic content:

| | | | |
|---|---|---|---|
| 1 | *Café* | 6 | *Sur-goutte* |
| 2 | *Gloria* | 7 | *Rincette* |
| 3 | *Pousse Café* | 8 | *Re-rincette* |
| 4 | *Goutte* | 9 | *Sur-rincette* |
| 5 | *Regoutte* | 10 | *Coup de l'étrier* |

## COUNTING FRUIT STONES

*When shall I marry?*
This year, next year, sometime, never.
*What will my husband be?*
Tinker, tailor, soldier, sailor, rich-man, poor-man, beggar-man, thief.
*What shall I wear?*
Silk, satin, cotton, rags.
*How shall I get it?*
Given, borrowed, bought, stolen.
*How shall I get to church?*
Coach, carriage, wheelbarrow, cart.
*Where shall I live?*
Big house, little house, pig-sty, barn.

## WATER IN IDIOM

A flawed plan will *hold no water;* a plan that is exposed might be *dead in the water,* or risks being *blown out of the water;* whereas a plan that will stand close scrutiny is *watertight* – unless someone *pours cold water* over it. (And even if they do, it might just be *water off a duck's back.*) To *carry water to the river* is like taking coals to Newcastle, and while you can *lead a horse to water, you can't make it drink.* If you have *muddied the water* you might seek to *pour oil over troubled waters;* a true friend will seek always to be a *bridge over troubled water.* If you fail to *keep your head above water,* you may find yourself in *hot water* or *deep water* (not forgetting, of course, that *still waters run deep*). You may not take to a *backwater* like a *duck to water* – indeed you may feel like a *fish out of water.* However, since *much water will have flowed under the bridge* it is advisable simply to *tread water* and avoid the temptation to *throw the baby out with the bathwater.* Remember always that *blood is thicker than water, come hell or high-water.*

## BRIMMERS, BUMPERS, BUZZES, BACK-HANDERS, & BISHOPS

A BRIMMER is a glass so full that the wine touches the brim. However, the meniscus effect may still allow a few additional drops to be added. A BUMPER, by contrast, is a glass so full that the wine rises slightly in the middle of the glass. This nice distinction can be tested by placing a fragment of cork on the surface of the wine. With a brimmer, the cork will float to the edge; with a bumper it will remain in the centre. The customary way to raise a toast is with a bumper of wine – however, the glass must be absolutely full so as not to show any 'daylight' between the wine and the rim. Before proposing a toast, toast-masters used to warn:

*'Gentlemen, no daylights nor heeltaps!'*

[A 'heeltap' is the residue of wine at the bottom of a glass.]

The term BUZZ is employed (amongst other places) at some formal high-table desserts. Here the tradition is to serve oneself wine in turn; passing the decanter or bottle round the table to the left[†]. A buzz is the free glass of wine received if, at your turn, you finish a bottle without fully filling your glass. A BACK-HANDER is when a wine's clockwise passage is temporarily reversed to fill up a glass on the right. As Thackeray wrote:

*'I'll take a back-hander, as Clive don't seem to drink.'*
*– The Newcomes*

If the wine is obstructed in its passage round the table by some greedy or unobservant individual, it is the custom in some quarters to jog the diner's attention by asking: 'Do you know the BISHOP OF NORWICH?'

† Certain port decanters were made with round bases so that they could not be put down until they had travelled round every guest. Only once the decanter had gone completely round the table could it be placed in the host's special rest ('hogget').

## HOMER SIMPSON'S 'Mmms...'

Some of the things that have caused Homer Simpson to drool 'Mmm…':

| | |
|---|---|
| Mmm......................donuts | Mmm............organized crime |
| Mmm......................money | Mmm................urinal fresh |
| Mmm .....the Land of Chocolate | Mmm......unprocessed fishsticks |
| Mmm................invisible Cola | Mmm.......maca-ma-damia nuts |
| Mmm ....................free goo | Mmm...............elephant fresh |
| Mmm...............bowling fresh | Mmm .....................hog fat |
| Mmm.....................caramel | Mmm..........footlong chili dog |

## THE BANTING DIET

In his 1869 *Letter on Corpulence*, William Banting declared: 'Of all the parasites that affect humanity I do not know of, nor can I imagine, any more distressing than that of Obesity.' As one who suffered from obesity, Banting hoped 'to help those who happened to be afflicted as I was, for that corpulence was remediable I was well convinced'. Banting's diet was:

'For BREAKFAST, I take five to six ounces of either beef mutton, kidneys, broiled fish, bacon, or cold meat of any kind except pork or veal; a large cup of tea or coffee (without milk or sugar), a little biscuit, or one ounce of dry toast; making together six ounces solid, nine liquid.

For DINNER, five or six ounces of any fish except salmon, herrings, or eels, any meat except pork or veal, any vegetable except potato, parsnip, beetroot, turnip, or carrot, one ounce of dry toast, fruit out of a pudding not sweetened, any kind of poultry or game, and two or three glasses of good claret, sherry, or Madeira – champagne, port, and beer forbidden; making together ten to twelve ounces solid, and ten liquid.

For TEA, two or three ounces of cooked fruit, a rusk or two, and a cup of tea without milk or sugar; making two to four ounces solid, nine liquid.

For SUPPER, three or four ounces of meat or fish, similar to dinner, with a glass or two of claret or sherry and water; making four ounces solid and seven liquid.

For NIGHTCAP, if required, a tumbler of grog (gin, whisky, or brandy, without sugar) or a glass or two of claret or sherry.'

*By means of this diet, Banting claimed to have reduced his weight from 202lb to 150lb over a year. 'I am fully persuaded that thousands of our fellow men might profit equally by a similar course to mine', he said.*

So popular was this diet that its creator (a humble London cabinet-maker by trade) found notoriety – so much so that *bant, bantingism, banting,* and *bantingize* are all to be found in the Oxford English Dictionary.

## GRACE BEFORE MEAT

Some hae meat, and canna eat,
  And some wad eat that want it,
But we hae meat and we can eat,
  And sae the Lord be thankit.

— ROBERT BURNS, 'The Selkirk Grace', *c.*1790

## THE LOVING CUP RITUAL

Loving (or Grace) cups are large ornamental drinking vessels with two or more handles, occasionally given as prizes or in commemoration of some event. Traditionally, loving cups were filled with wine, ale, champagne, or the like and passed round a gathering for all to drink from. There are a number of historic rituals governing how loving cups are passed from person to person that are supposed to date back to the treacherous assassination of King Edward the Martyr (*c.*963–78), who was stabbed to death at Corfe Castle while drinking from a stirrup-cup. To prevent another such assault, those on either side of the drinker stand guard, as illustrated below. Here, B is facing A; C holds the Cup; D is facing E:

| A | B | C | D | E | F |
|---|---|---|---|---|---|
| sitting | <— | drinking | —> | sitting | sitting |

Now, assuming C has just drunk from the Cup, the sequence is:
B turns to C; C bows to B, who bows and sits down.
D turns to C; C bows to D, who bows back.
D takes the cup from C.
C then bows to D, who bows back.
C turns to face B.
D turns to E who stands up and bows to D.
D bows back to E; E turns to face F.
D faces forward, drinks from the cup, and wipes the rim.
Once this sequence has been completed, the table will look thus:

| A | B | C | D | E | F |
|---|---|---|---|---|---|
| sitting | sitting | <— | drinking | —> | sitting |

This elaborate procedure is continued until the Cup has passed round the the table. Those who, for whatever reason, do not wish to drink from the Loving Cup, may simply follow the procedure without actually imbibing.

## UK LABELLING GUIDELINES

'Fat free'.................................................contains ≤0·15g of fat per 100g
'Sugar free' .............................................contains ≤0·2g of sugar per 100g
'High fibre'..............................................contains ≥6g of fibre per 100g
'Low fat'..................................................contains ≤3g of fat per 100g
'Low sugar' ..............................................contains ≤5g of sugar per 100g
'Low sodium' ..........................................contains ≤40mg of sodium per 100g
'Reduced fat' ..........contains ≥25% less fat than the standard product
'Reduced sugar'.....contains ≥25% less sugar than the standard product

## TEA GRADING NOMENCLATURE

Numerous systems exist for the grading of tea – green tea alone has three nomenclatures: one for Japanese green tea, and two for Chinese green tea (domestic and export). 'Orthodox' grading takes into account leaf size, appearance, and quality. The following is a basic nomenclature for Whole Leaf orthodox grades (broken leaf, fannings, and dust have other codes):

| | |
|---|---|
| SFTGFOP | Special Finest Tippy Golden Flowery Orange Pekoe |
| FTGFOP | Finest Tippy Golden Flowery Orange Pekoe |
| TGFOP | Tippy Golden Flowery Orange Pekoe |
| GFOP | Golden Flowery Orange Pekoe |
| FOP | Flowery Orange Pekoe |
| OP | Orange Pekoe |
| FP | Flowery Pekoe |
| P | Pekoe |
| PS | Pekoe Souchong |

## DISMEMBER A HERON: CARVING TERMS

In 1508 Wynkyn de Worde printed *The Booke of Kervinge,* in which were tabulated the different carving terms to be employed for various animals. Thus one would *thigh* a woodcock, *sauce* a tench, and *disfigure* a peacock:

| carving term | animal | | |
|---|---|---|---|
| | | thigh | a pigeon |
| | | border | a pasty |
| break | a deer | thigh | a woodcock |
| lesche (leach) | a brawn | timber | a fire |
| rear | a goose | tire | an egg |
| lift | a swan | chine | a salmon |
| sauce | a capon | string | a lamprey |
| spoil | a hen | splat | a pike |
| frusche (frus, ? truss) | a chicken | sauce | a plaice |
| unbrace | a mallard | sauce | a tench |
| unlace | a coney | splay | a bream |
| dismember | a heron | side | a haddock |
| display | a crane | rusk | a barbel |
| disfigure | a peacock | culpon | a trout |
| unjoint | a bittern | fin | a chevin |
| untache | a curlew | tranesse | an eel |
| alay | a felande | tranch | a sturgeon |
| wing | a partridge | undertranch | a porpoise |
| wing | a quail | tame | a crab |
| mine | a plover | barb | a lobster |

—— SOME FILMS FEATURING CANNIBALISM ——

Silence of the Lambs (1991) · Soylent Green (1973) · Eating Raoul (1982)
Bad Taste (1988) · The Texas Chain Saw Massacre (1974) · Urban Flesh
(1999) · Cannibal Hookers (1987) · The Cook, The Thief, His Wife & Her
Lover (1989) · Cannibal Holocaust (1979) · Hannibal (2001) · Delicatessen
(1991) · The Rocky Horror Picture Show (1975) · Sweeney Todd (1939)
The Donner Party (1992) · Eat The Rich (1987) · I Drink Your Blood (1971)
Parents (1989) · Ravenous (1999) · Manhunter (1986) · Weekend (1967)
Alive (1993) · Lieutenant Pimple, King of Cannibal Islands (1914) · The
Undertaker & His Pals (1967) · Emmanuelle & the Last Cannibals (1977)

—— BREAKFAST QUOTATIONS ——

WINSTON CHURCHILL · My wife and I tried two or three times in the last forty years to have breakfast together, but it was so disagreeable we had to stop.

SOMERSET MAUGHAM · To eat well in England you should have breakfast three times a day.

P.G. WODEHOUSE · I hadn't the heart to touch my breakfast. I told Jeeves to drink it himself.

OSCAR WILDE · Only dull people are brilliant at breakfast.

JOHN GUNTHER · All happiness depends on a leisurely breakfast.

A.P. HERBERT · The critical period in matrimony is breakfast-time.

TRADITIONAL · Laugh before breakfast, you'll cry before supper.

CHARLES WHEELER · *(on the spy George Blake)* He smiled rather too much. He smiled at breakfast, you know.

MARLENE DIETRICH · Once a woman has forgiven her man, she must not reheat his sins for breakfast.

LEWIS CARROLL · Why, sometimes I've believed as many as six impossible things before breakfast.

—— UNCONSIDERED TRIFLES ——

It is ironic that the trifle – a pudding named after something trivial and of no importance – has catalysed so much debate. Sherry or no sherry? Fruit or no fruit? Cinnamon? Mace? Custard? Sponge? Biscuits? Jelly? Angelica? Glacé cherries? Hundreds and thousands? As Myrtle Allen notes in *The Ballymaloe Cookbook*: 'I once heard three men arguing about how to make the one-and-only authentic trifle. Each man's grandmother had made the trifle of his life, and each had made it differently.'

# ——— SAMUEL JOHNSON ON FOOD & DRINK ———

One of the disadvantages of wine is that it makes a man mistake words for thoughts.

Some people have a foolish way of not minding, or pretending not to mind, what they eat. For my part, I mind my belly very studiously, … for I look upon it that he who does not mind his belly, will hardly mind anything else.

This was a good dinner enough, to be sure: but it was not a dinner to ask a man to.

Claret is the liquor for boys; port for men; but he who aspires to be a hero must drink brandy. In the first place, brandy is most grateful to the palate; and then brandy will do soonest for a man what drinking can do for him. There are, indeed, few who are able to drink brandy. That is a power rather to be wished for than attained.

A man seldom thinks with more earnestness of any thing than he does of his dinner; and if he cannot get that well dressed, he should be suspected of inaccuracy in other things.

Melancholy, indeed, should be diverted by every means but drinking.

For my part, now, I consider supper as a turnpike through which one must pass, in order to get to bed.

I, Madam, who live at a variety of good tables, am a much better judge of cookery, than any person who has a very tolerable cook, but lives much at home; for his palate is gradually adapted to the taste of his cook: whereas, Madam, in trying by a wider range, I can more exquisitely judge.

A cucumber should be well sliced, and dressed with pepper and vinegar, and then thrown out, as good for nothing.

It is not very easy to fix the principles upon which mankind have agreed to eat some animals, and reject others; and as the principle is not evident, it is not uniform. That which is selected as delicate in one country, is by its neighbours abhorred as loathsome.

[*On a dish of roast mutton*] It is as bad as bad can be: it is ill-fed, ill-killed, ill-kept, and ill-drest.

BOSWELL: You must allow me, Sir, at least that [wine] produces truth; *in vino veritas*, you know, Sir.
JOHNSON: That would be useless to a man who knew he was not a liar when he was sober.

Sir, I have no objection to a man's drinking wine, if he can do it in moderation. I found myself apt to go to excess in it, and therefore … I thought it better not to return to it. Every man is to judge for himself, according to the effects which he experiences.

## MEASURING SPAGHETTI

The following diagram provides a rough indication of the amount of spaghetti required for different numbers of people. Simply place the spaghetti (end on) onto the page over the appropriate circle. The measures are based on a serving of 110g (*c.*4oz) of spaghetti per person.

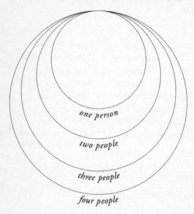

*one person*

*two people*

*three people*

*four people*

## SOME CULINARY PATRON SAINTS

| | |
|---|---|
| Animals ....... St Francis of Assisi | Dentists.............. St Apollonia |
| Bakers..................... St Zita | Fishermen............. St Andrew |
| Bee-keepers .......... St Ambrose | Grocers ................ St Michael |
| Cooks..... St Martha, St Laurence | Hoteliers ..... St Amand, St Julian |
| Dairymaids .............. St Brigid | Wine merchants ....... St Vincent |

## LARKS

Larks are small passerine birds that have traditionally been used in pies. Grimod de la Reynière dismissed the birds as 'a little bundle of toothpicks, more suitable for cleaning the mouth than filling it'. Indeed, so insignificant are larks that they were often weighed rather than counted. Queen Anne's physician, Dr Martin Lister, declared that, unless twelve larks weighed more than thirteen ounces, they should not be eaten. Legend has it that when Charles IX was released by his kidnappers from the forest of Orléans he promised to spare the lives of his captors on condition that they told him who created the lark pie he had been served.

## RDA & DRV

In 1991, Dietary Reference Values (DRV) replaced Recommended Daily Amounts (RDA) as the British government's preferred method of assessing individual diets. DRVs are benchmark intakes of energy and nutrients for healthy adults, which should be understood as guidance rather than exact recommendations. DRV is a general term which covers the following:

| EAR | RNI | LRNI | SAFE |
|---|---|---|---|
| *Estimated Average Requirement* | *Reference Nutrient Intake* | *Lower Reference Nutrient Intake* | INTAKE |
| The average quantity of a substance needed by a group. | The quantity of a substance required by around 97% of a group. | The quantity of a substance required for those in a group with the lowest need. | The lowest quantity of a substance required before the risk of undesirable effects. |

## THE FIVE TASTES

SALT · SWEET · SOUR · BITTER · UMAMI †

† Recently recognised, umami detects 'savoury' or 'meaty' sensations, and is stimulated by condiments like soy sauce, or by foods which contain glutamate compounds like MSG.

## BULIMIA & ANOREXIA

| BULIMIA NERVOSA | ANOREXIA NERVOSA |
|---|---|
| Sufferers consume large quantities of food, usually in a very short period of time, and then induce vomiting to purge themselves of the food they have eaten. | Sufferers believe, despite sometimes overwhelming evidence to the contrary, that they are overweight and, as a consequence, deny or starve themselves of food. |

## 57

The number 57 has been inexorably associated with the food giant Heinz ever since 1892 when the company's founder created the '57 Varieties' slogan. At the time, the company produced more than 57 products, but it seems that H(enry) J(ohn) Heinz (1844–1919) was inspired by an advert he saw for '21 styles of shoes' – as well as his curious faith in the numbers 5 and 7. (To this day, mail for the Heinz offices in Pittsburgh goes via P.O. Box 57, and the final digits of the Heinz phone number are 5757.)

## ───── ON WHEN TO DRINK CHAMPAGNE ─────

*I drink it when I am happy, and when I am sad.*
*Sometimes I drink it when I am alone.*
*When I have company, I consider it obligatory.*
*I trifle with it if I am not hungry, and drink it when I am.*
*Otherwise I never touch it – unless I am thirsty.*

— MADAME LILLY BOLLINGER [attrib.]

## ───── SOME KEY FOODS ON STAGE & SCREEN ─────

| | | |
|---|---|---|
| Apple strudel | *The Four Seasons* · | Arnold Wesker |
| Baby (see also p.20) | *Blasted* · | Sarah Kane |
| Blancmange | *The Glass Menagerie* · | Tennessee Williams |
| Borscht | *The Battleship Potemkin* · | Sergei Eisenstein |
| Breakfast | *Juno and the Paycock* · | Sean O'Casey |
| Butter | *Last Tango in Paris* · | Bernardo Bertolucci |
| Chickens, fried (four) | *The Blues Brothers* · | John Landis |
| Chocolate | *Chocolat* · | Lasse Hallström |
| Cucumber sandwiches | *The Importance of Being Earnest* · | Oscar Wilde |
| Eggs, scrambled | *The Absence of War* · | David Hare |
| Haggis | *The Gentle Shepherd* · | Allan Ramsay |
| Ham | *Jamon Jamon* · | J.J. Bigas Luna |
| Liver | *Brighton Beach Memoirs* · | Neil Simon |
| Mint (wafer thin) | *The Meaning of Life* · | Monty Python |
| Noodles | *Tampopo* · | Juzo Itami |
| Pork | *A Private Function* · | Malcolm Mowbray |
| Porridge | *The Jew of Malta* · | Christopher Marlow |
| Potato salad | *A Young Man's Grown-up Daughter* · | Viktor Slavkins |
| Quail with truffles | *Babette's Feast* · | Gabriel Axel |
| Ragu | *Saturday, Sunday, Monday* · | Eduardo De Filippo |
| Sardines | *Noises Off* · | Michael Frayn |
| Seafood | *Vatel* · | Roland Joffé (see p.101) |
| Snails | *Pretty Woman* · | Garry Marshall |
| Soda bread | *Dancing at Lughnasa* · | Brian Friel |
| Spaghetti | *Skylight* · | David Hare |

## ───── MICROBIAL COUNT IN RAW MEAT ─────

| *Microbial count (per g)* | *quality* | | |
|---|---|---|---|
| $10^2$ | Excellent condition | $10^6$ | rejected commercially |
| $10^4$ | good, commercial quality | $10^8$ | meat smells |
| | | $10^9$ | meat is slimy |

## NEW LABOUR & GRANITA

Tony Blair's premiership has been dogged by the rumour that he made a clandestine deal with Gordon Brown to hand over (eventually) the reins of power. It is claimed that this deal was struck at Granita – an Italian restaurant in Islington, North London, on 31 May 1994. Unfortunately, Granita has no record of that menu, but the restaurant's 1994 entry in Fay Maschler's *London Restaurant Guide* gives some notion of their meal:

> *This stark, fundamentally Italian restaurant has been a hit since it opened in the autumn of 1992 ... the menu is short, but has enough choice ... to give you an idea of the style – small pizza with aubergine and sun-dried tomato purée, roasted red pepper with rocket, oregano and a garlic vinaigrette, chargrilled organic salmon, roast chump of lamb with flageolets, floating islands with berry compote.*

Assuming they both had 3 courses and shared a bottle of wine, the meal would have cost Blair and Brown about £22 each – though it could be argued that, in the long run, the cost to Gordon Brown was far greater.

## TYPICAL CURRY POWDER FORMULATION

| Ground ingredient | range % | | |
|---|---|---|---|
| Coriander | 10–50 | Cinnamon | 0–5 |
| Cumin | 5–20 | Nutmeg | 0–5 |
| Turmeric | 10–35 | Clove | 0–5 |
| Fenugreek | 5–20 | Caraway | 0–5 |
| Ginger | 5–20 | Fennel | 0–5 |
| Celery | 0–15 | Cardamom | 0–5 |
| Black pepper | 0–10 | Salt | 0–10 |

(Tainter & Grenis, *Spices & Seasonings*, 1993)

## SALMAGUNDI

*Take a little cold veal, or cold fowl, the white part, free of fat and skin, mince it very fine; take either a red herring, a pickled herring, or three or four anchovies, which[ever] you please; if herring, skin and bone it; peel and shred small a couple of onions, core, pare, and shred two apples, a little hung beef mined fine. Lay it on a dish in small heaps, each ingredient separate; put a few anchovies into the middle of the dish. Garnish with lemon. Eat with oil, mustard, and vinegar.*

— Elizabeth Taylor, *The Art of Cookery*, 1769

---------- DINING ALONE ----------

Solitary dinners, I think, ought to be avoided as much as possible, because solitude tends to produce thought, and thought tends to the suspension of the digestive powers. When, however, dining alone is necessary, the mind should be disposed to cheerfulness by a previous interval of relaxation from whatever has seriously occupied the attention, and by directing it to some agreeable object.

— THOMAS WALKER, *c.*1835

--------- SOME AUSTRALIAN BEER GLASS SIZES ---------

Northern Territory
*Handle* (10oz/300ml)
*Schooner* (15oz/450ml)

Queensland
*Pot* (10oz/300ml)
*Schooner* (15oz/450ml)
*Jug* (40oz/1200ml)

Western Australia
*Glass* (7oz/210ml)
*Middie* (10oz/300ml)
*Pint* (20oz/600ml)

New South Wales
*Middie* (10oz/300ml)
*Schooner* (15oz/450ml)

South Australia
*Butcher* (7oz/210ml)
*Schooner* (10oz/300ml)
*Pint* (15oz/450ml)

*(Variations exist across Australia.)*

Victoria
*Glass* (7oz/210ml)
*Pot* (10oz/300ml)

Tasmania
*Six* (6oz/180ml)
*Eight* (8oz/240ml)
*Ten* (10oz/300ml)
*Pint* (20oz/600ml)

----------------- IRISH CHAMP -----------------

Champ is a traditional Northern Irish dish of rich, creamy mashed potatoes into which are added chopped spring onions and melted butter.

---SERVANTS' WAGES---

In 1825 Samuel and Sarah Adams published *The Complete Servant* – a detailed and influential 'manual of duty and practice' intended both for servants and their masters. Alongside a wealth of practical information ('to restore flat wines', 'to relieve an apoplectic fit', 'to clean Japanned candlesticks' [see p.74]) is an account of the duties and wages of staff. The number of servants needed for each establishment would depend on the size and income of the household. The Adams created a scale that ranged from a widow on 100 guineas a year – who would probably employ only a single maid servant; to a gentleman and lady with three children and an income of £5000, a household which could employ a staff of twenty-four:

> *A Housekeeper, Cook, Lady's-Maid, Nurse, two House-Maids, Laundry Maid, Still-Room Maid, Nursery-Maid, Kitchen Maid, and Scullion, with Butler, Valet, House-Steward, Coachman, two Grooms, one Assistant Groom, two Footmen, three Gardeners, and a Labourer.*

The annual wages (usually in guineas) servants could expect to earn were:

| FEMALE SERVANTS | | MALE SERVANTS | |
|---|---|---|---|
| Housekeeper | 25–50 | House-Steward | £100-£250 |
| Still-room maid | 8–12 | Steward's Room Boy | £8–£12 |
| Cook | *varied* | Butler | £50–80 |
| Kitchen Maid | 12–14 | Under Butler | 16–25 |
| Scullion, Scullery-Maid | 8–12 | Valet | £30–£60 |
| The Lady's-Maid | 18–25 | Footman | 20–30 |
| Head Nurse | 18–25 | Lady's-Footman | 18–25 |
| Under Nurse | 10–12 | Under-Footman | 16–20 |
| Nursery Maid | 6–10 | Hall Porter | 24–30 |
| Governess | 25–100 | Head Coachman | 25–26 |
| Upper House-Maid | 12–16 | Under Coachman | 20–24 |
| Under House-Maid | 10–12 | Groom | 22–25 |
| Servant of All Work | 8–12 | Stable Boy | £8–£21 |
| Laundry Maid | £8–£15 | Head Gardener | £50–£100 |
| Dairy Maid | £8–£12 | Under Gardener | 16–20*s. per week* |

*(The purchasing power of £1 in 1825 would be approximately equal to £45 in current money.)*

Depending on their station and seniority, servants expected various tips and perquisites in addition to their salary. For example, a Nursery Maid might be tipped after a baptism, and Butlers would expect to receive cast-off clothing from their masters, remainders of the wax candles, second-hand playing cards, and so on. Some employees (such as groom, valet, coachman, footman, and porter) would receive their uniforms for free.

## —— BRILLAT-SAVARIN'S RULES FOR DINING——

*'…But the impatient reader will probably exclaim how … is a dinner to be regulated so as to bring together all the requisites necessary to the highest pleasures of the table?*

Let not the number of the company exceed twelve, that the conversation may be constantly general.

Let them be so selected that their occupations are various, and their tastes analogous, and with such points of contact that there will be no need for the odious formality of presentations.

Let the dining-room be well lighted, the cloth spotless, and the atmosphere at a temperature from 13–16º Réaumur (60–68ºF).

Let the men have wit without pretension, and the women pleasant without being coquettes.

Let the dishes be exceedingly choice, but few in number: and the wines of the highest quality each in its degree.

Let the order of service be from the more substantial dishes to the lighter, and the simpler wines to the most perfumed.

Let the meal proceed without undue haste, since dinner is the last business of the day; and let the guests consider themselves as travellers about to reach a shared destination together.

Let the coffee be hot, and the liquors chosen with special care.

Let the drawing room be large enough to admit a game of cards for those who cannot do without it, while leaving ample room for post-prandial conversation.

Let the guests be detained by the charms of society, and animated by the hope that the evening will yet develop.

Let the tea not be too strong, the toast skilfully buttered, and the punch carefully prepared.

Let none leave before eleven o'clock, but let all be in bed by midnight.

*Whoever has been a guest at a repast combining all these conditions, may boast of having taken part at his own apotheosis.'*

Translated from Brillat-Savarin's
*La Physiologie du goût*, 1825

## ——W.H.O. DRINKING WATER STANDARDS——

| *Maximum permissible concentrations (mg/l)* | |
|---|---|
| Chlorides......................60 | Calcium.......................200 |
| Sulphates.....................400 | Magnesium ...................150 |
| | Total dissolved solids .......1,500 |

# THE BODY MASS INDEX

*Weight – lbs at the top, Kg at the bottom (conversions have been rounded)*

| height (inches) | 245 | 240 | 235 | 230 | 225 | 220 | 215 | 210 | 205 | 200 | 195 | 190 | 185 | 180 | 175 | 170 | 165 | 160 | 155 | 150 | 145 | 140 | 135 | 130 | 125 | 120 | height (cm) |
|---|---|---|---|---|---|---|---|---|---|---|---|---|---|---|---|---|---|---|---|---|---|---|---|---|---|---|---|
| 4'10" | ◉ | ◉ | ◉ | ◉ | ◉ | ◉ | ◉ | ◉ | ◉ | ◉ | ◉ | ◉ | ◉ | ◉ | ◉ | ◉ | ◉ | ◉ | ◉ | ◉ | ◉ | ⊙ | ⊙ | ⊙ | ⊙ | ⊙ | 147 |
| 4'11" | ◉ | ◉ | ◉ | ◉ | ◉ | ◉ | ◉ | ◉ | ◉ | ◉ | ◉ | ◉ | ◉ | ◉ | ◉ | ◉ | ◉ | ◉ | ◉ | ◉ | ⊙ | ⊙ | ⊙ | ⊙ | ⊙ | ○ | 150 |
| 5' | ◉ | ◉ | ◉ | ◉ | ◉ | ◉ | ◉ | ◉ | ◉ | ◉ | ◉ | ◉ | ◉ | ◉ | ◉ | ◉ | ◉ | ◉ | ◉ | ⊙ | ⊙ | ⊙ | ⊙ | ⊙ | ○ | ○ | 152 |
| 5'1" | ◉ | ◉ | ◉ | ◉ | ◉ | ◉ | ◉ | ◉ | ◉ | ◉ | ◉ | ◉ | ◉ | ◉ | ◉ | ◉ | ◉ | ◉ | ⊙ | ⊙ | ⊙ | ⊙ | ⊙ | ○ | ○ | ○ | 155 |
| 5'2" | ◉ | ◉ | ◉ | ◉ | ◉ | ◉ | ◉ | ◉ | ◉ | ◉ | ◉ | ◉ | ◉ | ◉ | ◉ | ◉ | ◉ | ⊙ | ⊙ | ⊙ | ⊙ | ⊙ | ○ | ○ | ○ | ○ | 157 |
| 5'3" | ◉ | ◉ | ◉ | ◉ | ◉ | ◉ | ◉ | ◉ | ◉ | ◉ | ◉ | ◉ | ◉ | ◉ | ◉ | ◉ | ⊙ | ⊙ | ⊙ | ⊙ | ⊙ | ○ | ○ | ○ | ○ | ○ | 160 |
| 5'4" | ◉ | ◉ | ◉ | ◉ | ◉ | ◉ | ◉ | ◉ | ◉ | ◉ | ◉ | ◉ | ◉ | ◉ | ⊙ | ⊙ | ⊙ | ⊙ | ⊙ | ⊙ | ○ | ○ | ○ | ○ | ○ | ○ | 163 |
| 5'5" | ◉ | ◉ | ◉ | ◉ | ◉ | ◉ | ◉ | ◉ | ◉ | ◉ | ◉ | ◉ | ◉ | ◉ | ⊙ | ⊙ | ⊙ | ⊙ | ⊙ | ○ | ○ | ○ | ○ | ○ | ○ | ○ | 165 |
| 5'6" | ◉ | ◉ | ◉ | ◉ | ◉ | ◉ | ◉ | ◉ | ◉ | ◉ | ◉ | ◉ | ◉ | ⊙ | ⊙ | ⊙ | ⊙ | ⊙ | ⊙ | ○ | ○ | ○ | ○ | ○ | ○ | ○ | 167 |
| 5'7" | ◉ | ◉ | ◉ | ◉ | ◉ | ◉ | ◉ | ◉ | ◉ | ◉ | ◉ | ⊙ | ⊙ | ⊙ | ⊙ | ⊙ | ⊙ | ⊙ | ○ | ○ | ○ | ○ | ○ | ○ | ○ | ○ | 170 |
| 5'8" | ◉ | ◉ | ◉ | ◉ | ◉ | ◉ | ◉ | ◉ | ◉ | ◉ | ⊙ | ⊙ | ⊙ | ⊙ | ⊙ | ⊙ | ⊙ | ○ | ○ | ○ | ○ | ○ | ○ | ○ | ○ | ○ | 173 |
| 5'9" | ◉ | ◉ | ◉ | ◉ | ◉ | ◉ | ◉ | ◉ | ◉ | ⊙ | ⊙ | ⊙ | ⊙ | ⊙ | ⊙ | ⊙ | ○ | ○ | ○ | ○ | ○ | ○ | ○ | ○ | ○ | ○ | 175 |
| 5'10" | ◉ | ◉ | ◉ | ◉ | ◉ | ◉ | ◉ | ⊙ | ⊙ | ⊙ | ⊙ | ⊙ | ⊙ | ⊙ | ○ | ○ | ○ | ○ | ○ | ○ | ○ | ○ | ○ | ○ | ○ | ○ | 178 |
| 5'11" | ◉ | ◉ | ◉ | ◉ | ◉ | ◉ | ⊙ | ⊙ | ⊙ | ⊙ | ⊙ | ⊙ | ⊙ | ⊙ | ○ | ○ | ○ | ○ | ○ | ○ | ○ | ○ | ○ | ○ | ○ | ○ | 180 |
| 6' | ◉ | ◉ | ◉ | ◉ | ◉ | ⊙ | ⊙ | ⊙ | ⊙ | ⊙ | ⊙ | ⊙ | ⊙ | ○ | ○ | ○ | ○ | ○ | ○ | ○ | ○ | ○ | ○ | ○ | ○ | ○ | 183 |
| 6'1" | ◉ | ◉ | ◉ | ◉ | ⊙ | ⊙ | ⊙ | ⊙ | ⊙ | ⊙ | ⊙ | ⊙ | ○ | ○ | ○ | ○ | ○ | ○ | ○ | ○ | ○ | ○ | ○ | ○ | ○ | ○ | 185 |
| 6'2" | ◉ | ◉ | ◉ | ⊙ | ⊙ | ⊙ | ⊙ | ⊙ | ⊙ | ⊙ | ○ | ○ | ○ | ○ | ○ | ○ | ○ | ○ | ○ | ○ | ○ | ⊕ | ⊕ | ⊕ | ⊕ | ⊕ | 188 |
| 6'3" | ◉ | ⊙ | ⊙ | ⊙ | ⊙ | ⊙ | ⊙ | ⊙ | ⊙ | ⊙ | ○ | ○ | ○ | ○ | ○ | ○ | ○ | ○ | ○ | ○ | ⊕ | ⊕ | ⊕ | ⊕ | ⊕ | ⊕ | 190 |
| **Kg** | 111 | 108 | 106 | 104 | 102 | 100 | 97 | 95 | 93 | 91 | 88 | 86 | 84 | 82 | 79 | 77 | 75 | 73 | 70 | 68 | 66 | 63 | 61 | 59 | 57 | 54 | |

The Body Mass Index (BMI) is a measure of the healthy weight:height ratio. This table gives a broad-brush indication of adult BMI status. Match height along the vertical axis with weight along the horizontal axis to gauge your weight status: ⊕ = Underweight (BMI<18.5) · ○ = Normal (BMI=18.5–24.9) · ⊙ = Overweight (BMI = 25–29.9) · ◉ = Obese (BMI>30)

## SANSKRIT COOKING

Classic Sanskrit literature is said to enumerate eight methods of cooking:

| | |
|---|---|
| *thalanam* | drying |
| *kvathanam* | par-boiling |
| *pachanam* | cooking with water |
| *svedanam* or *svinnabhakshya* | steaming |
| *apakva* | frying |
| *bharjanam* | dry-roasting |
| *thanduram* | grilling |
| *putapaka* | baking |

## THIRTEEN AT TABLE

In many cultures the presence of thirteen at a dinner table is considered unlucky. In part this is due to the general superstitions which surround the number, yet it is clear that dining with thirteen is a special concern. The French used to hire an additional diner (or *Quartorzienne*) to make up the fourteenth place. At the Savoy Hotel, London, a wooden cat named Kaspar (carved by Basil Ionides, 1926) is set a place at table when a party of 13 sits down to eat. The most obvious source of these concerns must be the Last Supper when Jesus broke bread with his Apostles the night before his death. In ancient Norse mythology thirteen was considered unlucky after the events at a banquet in Valhalla where Baldur was slain after Loki had intruded, thus becoming the thirteenth diner.

## DELIA SMITH ON MICROWAVES

I truly have tried ... and we had a microwave to heat things in [during] the filming – but, actually, we mainly used it to keep the ashtrays in. I think it takes the soul out of food. — *The Times*, 1990

## PIMMS

PIMMS was concocted in 1823 by James Pimm to complement the oysters he served in his bar *The City of London*. Although the gin-based PIMMS No.1 CUP is the most enduring version of the drink, over the years six versions of PIMMS CUP have been made, each based on a different spirit:

| No.1 | gin | No.3 | brandy | No.5 | rye |
|---|---|---|---|---|---|
| No.2 | whisky | No.4 | rum | No.6 | vodka |

## TUSSER'S PERFECT CHEESE

In his elaborate text *Five Hundred Good Points of Husbandry* (1573), Thomas Tusser presents ten characteristics the perfect cheese must have:

1 ............. Not like Gehazi, i.e. dead white, like a leper............. 1
2 ....................... Not like Lot's wife, all salt ....................... 2
3 ..................... Not like Argus, full of eyes....................... 3
4 ............... Not like Tom Piper, 'hoven and puffed' ............... 4
5 ................. Not like Crispin, leathery ................. 5
6 ................... Not like Lazarus, poor ................... 6
7 ................. Not like Esau, hairy ................. 7
8 ......... Not like Mary Magdalene, full of whey or maudlin ......... 8
9 ................. Not like the Gentiles, full of maggots ................. 9
10 ............. Not like a Bishop, made of burnt milk ............. 10

## CAPTAIN NEMO'S LARDER

An extract from Jules Verne's *20,000 Leagues Under the Sea* where Captain Nemo replies to Prof. Aronnax's queries about food aboard the *Nautilus*:

> *'What you believe to be red meat, Professor, is nothing other than loin of sea turtle. Similarly, here are some dolphin livers you might mistake for stewed pork. My chef is a skilful food processor who excels at pickling and preserving these various exhibits from the ocean. Feel free to sample all of these foods. Here are some preserves of sea cucumber that a Malaysian would declare to be unrivaled in the entire world, here's cream from milk furnished by the udders of cetaceans, and sugar from the huge fucus plants in the North Sea; and finally, allow me to offer you some marmalade of sea anemone, equal to that from the tastiest fruits.'*

> *So I sampled away, more as a curiosity seeker than an epicure, while Captain Nemo delighted me with his incredible anecdotes.*

## SPICES, FIVE AND FOUR

| FOUR SPICE | FIVE SPICE |
| --- | --- |
| ground pepper | star anise |
| nutmeg | clove |
| cloves | fennel |
| ginger | cinnamon |
| *(occasionally cinnamon)* | Sichuan pepper |

—————— SOME NOTABLE APPLES ——————

❦ The APPLES OF PYBAN were wild apples which, according to Sir John Mandeville, were able to sustain the pygmies on the Island of Pyban (or Pytan) simply by their odour. ❦ *The Arabian Nights* tells of PRINCE AHMED'S APPLE, purchased at Samarkand, which had the powers of a panacea. ❦ The APPLES OF SODOM were the fruit of the trees that grow on the banks of the Dead Sea, which turned to ashes in the mouth. Lord Byron wrote in *Childe Harold:* 'Like to the apples on the Dead Sea's shore; All ashes to the taste'. ❦ Scandinavian mythology tells of the GOLDEN APPLES OF IDUNA (the wife of Bragi, God of poetry) which kept the Gods eternally youthful. ❦ TURING'S APPLE relates to Alan M. Turing (1912–54) – a pioneer of early computing who was awarded the OBE for his work on the Enigma code. In June 1954, having been exposed as a homosexual, Turing committed suicide apparently by eating an apple that he had impregnated with cyanide. It has been suggested that Apple Macintosh computers were so named in tribute to Turing. ❦ Tricked by the wicked Queen into eating a poisoned apple, SNOW WHITE falls into a deep sleep, to be awoken by the kiss of a handsome prince. ❦ ISAAC NEWTON, in addition to his lesser-known roles as Master of the Mint and MP, is said to have discovered the law of gravitation by watching an apple fall to the ground. The tree was located in Woolsthorpe Manor, near Grantham, and it is claimed that the apple in question might have been the pyriform cooker known as *Flower of Kent.* ❦ The ADAM'S APPLE (or laryngeal prominence) is the thyroid cartilage surrounding the voice box [larynx] at the top of the windpipe [trachea]. It is said to be named after the piece of forbidden fruit which stuck in Adam's throat. ❦ THE HESPERIDES were daughters of Atlas who lived in a fabulous garden in the extreme West. There, aided by the hundred-headed serpent Ladon, they guarded the golden fruit of an apple tree – the wedding gift of Gaia to Hera. As one of his labours Hercules stole the apples, only for Athena later to return them. ❦ One of the few legendary crossbow marksmen, WILLIAM TELL (*c.*1250) was a Swiss patriot who defended Bürglen against Austrian oppression. Legend has it that the Austrian governor Hermann Gessler forced Tell to shoot an apple off his son's head at a distance of 80 paces. Tell performed this feat and later took his revenge by killing Gessler. ❦ The APPLE OF DISCORD (inscribed 'For the Fairest') was thrown by Eris, the personification of Strife, into a gathering of the Gods at the marriage of Thetis and Peleus. Hera (Juno), Athene (Minerva) and Aphrodite (Venus) all claimed ownership of the apple, and Paris was asked to judge which of the three was worthy (hence 'the Judgement of Paris'). Paris chose Aphrodite, who promised him the beautiful Helen, thus precipitating the downfall of Troy. ❦ The ruby-coloured SINGING APPLE OF LIBYA, guarded by a three-headed twelve-footed dragon, could impart any faculty (wit, wisdom, etc.) to those who smelt its odour. ❦

## EGG SIZES

### TRADITIONAL UK SIZES

| | | | |
|---|---|---|---|
| Size 0 | >75g | Size 4 | 55–60g |
| Size 1 | 70–75g | Size 5 | 50–55g |
| Size 2 | 65–70g | Size 6 | 45–50g |
| Size 3 | 60–65g | Size 7 | <45g |

### MODERN UK SIZES

| | | | |
|---|---|---|---|
| Very Large (XL) | >73g | Medium (M) | 53–63g |
| Large (L) | 63–73g | Small (S) | <53g |

### AMERICAN SIZES
*(minimum net weight per dozen)*

| | | | |
|---|---|---|---|
| Jumbo | >30oz | Medium | >21oz |
| Extra Large | >27oz | Small | >18oz |
| Large | >24oz | Peewee | >15oz |

## SUPERNACULAR

SUPERNACULAR · *adjective* · A description of wine so superlative that it is drunk to the very last drop – proved by upturning the empty glass upon one's finger-nail and ensuring that not a single drop forms thereon.

*Some of the finer kinds [of sherry] are really supernacular,*
*the best Tio Pepe for instance* — G. Saintsbury, 1920

## QUOTES ON LUNCH

ALDOUS HUXLEY · A man may be a pessimistic determinist before lunch and an optimistic believer in the will's freedom after it.

GERALD FORD · The 3-Martini lunch is the epitome of American efficiency. Where else can you get an earful, a bellyful and a snootful at the same time?

GORDON GEKKO · Lunch? You gotta be kidding. Lunch is for wimps.    [Attributed to Oliver Stone]

LORD CURZON · Gentlemen do not take soup at luncheon.

LORENZO DI COMO · Without lunch, what will become of love?

RAYMOND SOKOLOV · Manhattan is a narrow island off the coast of New Jersey devoted to the pursuit of lunch.

ANONYMOUS · There's no such thing as a free lunch. [Used as a book title by the economist Milton Friedman]

## pH OF SOME FOODS

| | | | |
|---|---|---|---|
| Lemons | 2·3–2·6 | Potatoes | 5·4–5·8 |
| Vinegar | 2·4–2·8 | White bread | 5·4–5·5 |
| Wine | 2·8–3·2 | Meats | 5·5–6·5 |
| Apples | 3·0–3·3 | Cauliflower | 5·6–5·7 |
| Oranges | 3·2–3·8 | Hard cheese | 5·6–6·2 |
| Peaches | 3·4–3·6 | Sardines | 6·2–6·4 |
| Yoghurt | 4·0–4·5 | Poultry | 6·4–6·6 |
| Beer | 4·1–4·3 | Milk | 6·5–6·7 |
| Black coffee | 5·0–5·1 | [Saliva = 6·3–6·4 · Neutral = 7·0] | |

## WINE LORE

The French have a number of traditional proverbs classifying wine by the effect they have on the drinker. These seem to be based, in part, on the Talmudic parable of Noah's vineyard, where Satan spied Noah planting his vines and offered to help. Satan slaughtered a lamb, a lion, a monkey, a pig, and poured their blood over the vine. Satan's message was that with one glass of wine man was like a lamb, gentle and mild; with two glasses he becomes like a lion, full of pride; with three glasses he becomes like a monkey, chattering and profane; and when drunk, man becomes like a pig, wallowing in his own shame. It is possible that Chaucer was alluding to this parable, or a similar story, when he wrote in *The Manciple's Tale:*

> 'I trow that ye have drunken wine of ape,
> And that is when men playe with a straw'

| *Wine that makes you...* | | | |
|---|---|---|---|
| Stupid | *vin d'âne* | Talkative | *vin de pie* |
| Maudlin, tearful | *vin de cerf* | Crafty | *vin de renard* |
| Quarrelsome | *vin de lion* | Rude, troublesome | *vin de singe* |
| | | Sick | *vin de porc* |

Along similar lines, and perhaps inspired by the same parable, in 1592 Thomas Nash proposed a menagerie of the eight degrees of drunkenness:

> The Ape-drunk, who leaps and sings and hollers
> The Lion-drunk, who is quarrelsome and rude
> The Swine-drunk, who is sleepy and lumpish
> The Sheep-drunk, wise in his own conceit, but unable to speak
> The Maudlin-drunk, who declares he loves all mankind
> The Martin-drunk, who drinks himself sober again
> The Goat-drunk, who is lascivious
> The Fox-drunk, who is crafty, like the Dutch who bargain when drunk

## SLAVES AT A ROMAN FEAST

Alexis Soyer's 1853 *Pantropheon* gives a taxonomy of slaves at a Roman feast. Each slave (branded with the mark of his master) had a specific role:

*dispensator* . . . . . . . . . . . . . . . . . organised the other slaves; apportioned work
*ostiarius* . . . . . . . . . . . . . . . . . porter who oversaw all who entered and exited
*atriensis* . . . . . . . . . . . . . . supervised the atrium; guarded arms, trophies, etc.
*obsonator* . . . . . . . . . purchased meat, fruit, and delicacies from the market
*vocatores* . . . . . . . . . . . . delivered invitations; received and placed the guests
*cubicularii* . . . . . . . . . . . . . . . . . . . . . . . . . . . . . . arranged the tables and couches
*dapiferi* . . . . . . . . . . . . . . . . . . . . . . . brought the dishes into the dining room
*nomenculatores* . . . . . . . . . . informed the guests of the qualities of each dish
*structor* . . . . . . . . . . . . . . . . . . . . . . . . . . . . . . . . arranged the dishes symmetrically
*praegustator* . . . . . . . . . . . . . . . . . . . . . . . . chief taster who sampled every dish
*triclinarche* . . . . . . . . . . . chief steward who oversaw the progress of the meal
*procillatores* . . . . . . . . . . . . . young slaves who attended to each guest's needs
*sandaligeruli* . . . . . . . . . . . . . . . . . . . . removed and replaced the guests' sandals
*adversitores* . . . . . . . . . . . . . . . . . . . . . conducted the guests home by torchlight

In addition were slaves who attended to the entertainment of the guests, as well as a host of more menial slaves: *flabellarii,* who cooled the guests with peacocks' feathers; *focarii,* who attended to the fires; *scoparii,* who swept the apartments; and *peniculi,* who cleaned the banqueting tables.

## ULLAGE

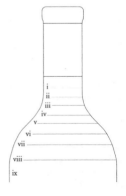

Ullage is the term employed to describe the amount of space in a wine bottle, not filled with wine. A range of naming systems exists to classify ullage levels – one of which is:

i . . . . . . . . . . . . . . . . . . . . . . . . . . . . . . . . into neck
ii . . . . . . . . . . . . . . . . . . . . . . . . . . . . bottom-neck
iii . . . . . . . . . . . . . . . . . . . . . . . . very top-shoulder
iv . . . . . . . . . . . . . . . . . . . . . . . . . . . . top-shoulder
v . . . . . . . . . . . . . . . . . . . . . . . . . . upper-shoulder
vi . . . . . . . . . . . . . . . . . . . . . . . . . . . . mid-shoulder
vii . . . . . . . . . . . . . . . . . . . . . . mid-low-shoulder
viii . . . . . . . . . . . . . . . . . . . . . . . . . . . low-shoulder
ix . . . . . . . . . . . . . . . . . . . . . . below low-shoulder

In naval slang, *ullage* was employed to describe an entire crew as useless.

## ——————— ADDRESS TO THE HAGGIS ———————

Composed by Robert Burns, *c*.1786, in the Standard-Habbie stanza form.

> Fair fa' your honest, sonsie face,
> Great chieftain o' the puddin'-race!
> Aboon them a' ye tak your place,
>     Painch, tripe, or thairm:
> Weel are ye wordy o' a grace
>     As lang's my arm.
>
> The groaning trencher there ye fill,
> Your hurdies like a distant hill,
> Your pin was help to mend a mill
>     In time o' need,
> While thro' your pores the dews distil
>     Like amber bead.
>
> His knife see rustic Labour dight,
> An' cut you up wi' ready sleight,
> Trenching your gushing entrails bright,
>     Like ony ditch;
> And then, O what a glorious sight,
>     Warm-reekin', rich!
>
> Then, horn for horn, they stretch an' strive:
> Deil tak the hindmost! on they drive,
> Till a' their weel-swall'd kytes belyve
>     Are bent like drums;
> Then auld Guidman, maist like to rive,
>     'Bethanket!' hums.
>
> Is there that owre his French *ragout*
> Or *olio* that wad staw a sow,
> Or *fricassee* wad mak her spew
>     Wi' perfect sconner,
> Looks down wi' sneering, scornfu' view
>     On sic a dinner?
>
> Poor devil! see him owre his trash,
> As feckless as wither'd rash,
> His spindle shank, a guid whip-lash,
>     His nieve a nit;
> Thro' blody flood or field to dash,
>     O how unfit!

## ADDRESS TO THE HAGGIS cont.

But mark the Rustic, haggis-fed,
The trembling earth resounds his tread,
Clap in his walie nieve a blade,
     He'll mak it whissle;
An' legs an' arms, an' heads will sned,
     Like taps o' trissle.


Ye Pow'rs wha mak mankind your care,
And dish them out their bill o' fare,
Auld Scotland wants nae skinking ware
     That jaups in luggies;
But, if ye wish her gratefu' prayer,
     Gie her a Haggis!

## THE PHILOSOPHER'S EGG AND OTHER PROTECTORS FROM POISON

A panacea, protector from plague, and preservative against poison, the Philosopher's Egg is made by pricking the shell of a fresh egg and blowing out the contents. The egg is then refilled with saffron, or saffron blended with the yolk. (In a different context, the Philosopher's Egg is a curious piece of curved glassware said to be employed in the practice of alchemy.) Legend tells of many other objects which could protect against poison:

Aladdin's ring ..................................... *protected against all evils*
Opals ................................... *turn pale in the presence of poison*
The Gate of Gundoforus... *through which none could pass carrying poison*
Rhinoceros's horns.............. *cause poison poured into them to effervesce*
Nourgehan's bracelet..... *the stones of which trembled when near to poison*
Venetian glass ........................... *will crack if poison is poured into it*
Unicorn horns ........................... *cause poisonous plants to wither*
[See also: Mithridatization, p.50; Dangerous Food, p.72; Bezoars, p.116; Fugu, p.138.]

## PARMENTIER

Antoine A. Parmentier (1737–1813) was the French agriculturalist credited with improving the production and popularising the eating of potatoes. Parmentier presented potatoes to the French Court in 1785 in an attempt to persuade the king of the benefits of potatoes to the general population. (Upon him was bestowed the singular honour of kissing Marie Antoinette's hand.) Dishes containing potato are described as *Parmentier*.

—————— BIBLICAL FOOD ABOMINATIONS ——————

Extracts from Leviticus, Chapter 11, the Authorised King James Version:

1 And the LORD spake unto Moses and to Aaron, saying unto them,

2 SPEAK unto the children of Israel, saying, These *are* the beasts which ye shall eat among all the beasts that are on the earth.

3 Whatsoever parteth the hoof, and is clovenfooted, *and* cheweth the cud, among the beasts, that shall ye eat.

4 Nevertheless these shall ye not eat of them that chew the cud, or of them that divide the hoof: *as* the camel, because he cheweth the cud, but divideth not the hoof; he *is* unclean unto you.

5 And the coney, because he cheweth the cud, but divideth not the hoof; he *is* unclean unto you.

6 And the hare, because he cheweth the cud, but divideth not the hoof; he *is* unclean unto you.

7 And the swine, though he divide the hoof, and be clovenfooted, yet he cheweth not the cud; he *is* unclean to you.

8 Of their flesh shall ye not eat, and their carcase shall ye not touch; they *are* unclean to you.

9 These shall ye eat of all that *are* in the waters: whatsoever hath fins and scales in the waters, in the seas, and in the rivers, them shall ye eat.

10 And all that have not fins and scales in the seas, and in the rivers, of all that move in the waters, and of any living thing which *is* in the waters, they *shall be* an abomination unto you:

11 They shall be even an abomination unto you; ye shall not eat of their flesh, but ye shall have their carcases in abomination.

12 Whatsoever hath no fins nor scales in the waters, that *shall be* an abomination unto you.

13 And these *are they which* ye shall have in abomination among the fowls; they shall not be eaten, they *are* an abomination: the eagle, and the ossifrage, and the ospray,

14 And the vulture, and the kite after his kind;

15 Every raven after his kind;

16 And the owl, and the night hawk, and the cuckow, and the hawk after his kind,

17 And the little owl, and the cormorant, and the great owl,

18 And the swan, and the pelican, and the gier eagle,

19 And the stork, the heron after her kind, and the lapwing, and the bat.

20 All fowls that creep, going upon *all* four, *shall be* an abomination unto you.

21 Yet these may ye eat of every flying creeping thing that goeth upon *all* four, which have legs above their feet, to leap withal upon the earth;

22 *Even* these of them ye may eat; the locust after his kind, and the bald locust after his kind, and the beetle after his kind, and the grasshopper after his kind.

23 But all *other* flying creeping things, which have four feet, *shall be* an abomination unto you...

## BIBLICAL FOOD ABOMINATIONS

29 These also *shall be* unclean unto you among the creeping things that creep upon the earth; the weasel, and the mouse, and the tortoise after his kind,

30 And the ferret, and the chameleon, and the lizard, and the snail, and the mole...

41 And every creeping thing that creepeth upon the earth *shall be* an abomination; it shall not be eaten.

42 Whatsoever goeth upon the belly, and whatsoever goeth upon *all* four, or whatsoever hath more feet among all creeping things that creep upon the earth, them ye shall not eat; for they *are* an abomination...

44 For I *am* the LORD your God: ye shall therefore sanctify yourselves, and ye shall be holy; for I *am* holy: neither shall ye defile yourselves with any manner of creeping thing that creepeth upon the earth.

45 For I *am* the LORD that bringeth you up out of the land of Egypt, to be your God: ye shall therefore be holy, for I *am* holy.

46 This *is* the law of the beasts, and of the fowl, and of every living creature that moveth in the waters, and of every creature that creepeth upon the earth:

47 To make a difference between the unclean and the clean, and between the beast that may be eaten and the beast that may not be eaten.

## SOME SLANG FOR DRUNKENNESS

*Drunk · pissed · intoxicated · boozed-up · fuddled · muddled · reely · tipsy pissed · rat-faced · arseholed · cut · half-cut · rather hightitty · got a crumb in his beard · in his cups · got a skinful · taken draps · had his wig oil'd diddled · sees double · sloshed · wankered · reeled · bit by a barnmouse whittled · kisky · lushed · has a brick in 'is hat · has the mainbrace well spliced smells of the cork · sniffed the barmaid's apron · trolleyed · beagered · quisby queer · has a guest in the attic · pickled · well soused · overcome · pruned jug-bitten · obfuscated · cup-sprung · pot-valient · cannonaded · spiced drilled · taverned · tight · shit-faced · bitten by the brewer's horse · oinked hiccius-doccius · smashed · tired and emotional · lost his sea-legs · addled three-sheets-to-the-wind · having a drop of the sun in the eye · raddled (too) far gone · elephant's trunk · living in Liquorpond Street[†] · sherbetty fly-blown · sozzled · flushed · mashed · hammered · nailed · wet · screwed legless · has his soul in soak · nazy · speechless · sponged · paralytic · squiffy tangle-footed · soused · rosinned · spiffed · spooned · swiggled · swattled ramped · drowned · snookered · sauced · lamped · whipped · pontooned*

[†] Situated in London, near Gray's Inn and Leather Lane, Liquorpond Street was, in the C18th, home to a number of breweries. It was rebuilt as Clerkenwell Road in 1878.

## WINE BOTTLE NOMENCLATURE

| Bottle Name | Champagne | Bordeaux | Burgundy |
|---|---|---|---|
| Picolo | ¼ | NA | NA |
| Chopine | NA | ⅓ | NA |
| Filette / Demi | ½ | ½ | ½ |
| Magnum | 2 | 2 | 2 |
| Marie Jeanne | NA | 3 | NA |
| Double Magnum | NA | 4 | NA |
| Jeroboam | 4 | 6 | 4 |
| Rehoboam | 6 | NA | 6 |
| Imperial | NA | 8 | NA |
| Methuselah | 8 | NA | 8 |
| Salmanazar | 12 | NA | 12 |
| Balthazar | 16 | 16 | 16 |
| Nebuchadnezzar | 20 | 20 | 20 |
| Melchior | 24 | 24 | 24 |

### JEROBOAM

Jeroboam I (*c.*922–901BC) founded the Northern Kingdom of Israel, having previously been in charge of Solomon's taxes and slave labour. After Solomon's death, Jeroboam fought Solomon's son Rehoboam to gain control of the Northern lands. In an attempt to rival Jerusalem as the centre of pilgrimage, Jeroboam established shrines at Bethel and Dan, and appointed his own priests.

### REHOBOAM

Rehoboam was the son of King Solomon whose reign (*c.*922–915BC) saw the break-up of the monarchy, and the foundation of a new kingdom under Jeroboam I.

### METHUSELAH

The grandfather of Noah, who lived to the venerable age of 969.

### SALMANAZAR

A name probably derived from Shalmaneser III, who reigned as the King of Assyria (*c.*859–824BC). Shalmaneser attempted to increase Assyrian influence over the Levant.

### BALTHAZAR

One of the three Wise Men, Balthazar bought myrrh (a symbol of mortality) to the infant Jesus.

### NEBUCHADNEZZAR

Probably after the Babylonian king Nebuchadnezzar II (?630–562BC), who established a New Babylonian empire and built the wondrous Hanging Gardens of Babylon. He apparently went mad and ate grass.

### MELCHIOR

Another of the three Wise Men, Melchior bought the infant Jesus frankincense, a symbol of divinity.

*(Wine is usually matured in bottles no larger than a Magnum.)*

---- ASPARAGUS & URINE ----

Asparagus (*Asparagus officinalis*) is a perennial vegetable of the lily family that has been enjoyed at least since Greek times. Its name probably derives from the Persian for sprout, *asparag,* and in England it used to be known as *sperage,* and *sparrow-grass* – in the trade it is still referred to as *grass.* Whereas the Greeks ate wild asparagus, the Romans developed such a taste for the vegetable that they developed techniques to cultivate it. These techniques were copied across the Middle East and Europe, arriving in England by the mid-C16th. Louis XIV enjoyed asparagus (and other delicacies) so much that he encouraged his gardener Jean de la Quintinie to develop hotbeds in order that he could enjoy such vegetables throughout the year. It is not known when the link between asparagus and urine smelling of cabbage was first made, but John Arbuthnot, physician to Queen Anne, noted the effect in 1731. (The C19th writer Stanlislas Martin warned that asparagus in the urine might betray an adulterous liaison.) The scientific literature is by no means agreed as to the cause of the smell. It seems that not everyone's urine is affected. Statistical results differ, but as many as 40–70% of those tested after consuming asparagus have urine which smells. However, to complicate matters further, not all people can detect the smell of asparaginous urine. So, there seem to be four groups: the producers and non-producers, and the sensors and non-sensors. The chemical cause of asparagus's mephitic character is equally uncertain, and the finger has been pointed at a range of agents including dimethyl sulfone, methanethiol, dimethyl sulfide, and S-methylthioacrylate. Research continues into this vital medical question.

---- INDIAN FOOD MEASURES ----

Traditional Indian systems for measurement appear to relate to the weight of a small black seed which was marked with a red dot. This seed (*Abrus precatorius*) – variously called *rati, gunji,* or *krsnala* – weighs 109mg, and was part of a very natural series of measures, as the following table shows:

| | |
|---|---|
| 1 pepper seed | 1 black mustard seed [sic] |
| 3 black mustard seeds | 1 white mustard seed |
| 6 white mustard seeds | 1 middle-sized barley corn |
| 3 barley corns | 1 rati |
| 8 barley corns | 1 angula (finger's breadth) |
| 12 angulas | 1 vitasti |
| 2 vitastis | 1 hasta |
| 4 hastas | 1 danda (rod) |
| 2,000 dandas | 1 krosa (the distance a cry would carry) |
| 4 krosas | 1 yojana (a stage of travel) |

## SPORKS, WOONS, & RUNCIBLE SPOONS

The SPORK is a combination spoon and three-pronged fork, sometimes with a sharpened or serrated cutting edge. Although the term (a conflation of spoon and fork) was current in 1909, the spork was only patented in 1970 by the American Van Brode Milling Company. The WOON is, apparently, the name given to the curved wooden spatulas which come with small tubs of ice-cream. Edward Lear introduced the world to the RUNCIBLE SPOON in *The Owl and the Pussy Cat* (1871):

> *They dinèd on mince, and slices of quince,*
> *Which they ate with a runcible spoon.*

Opinion is divided as to what a runcible spoon might look like. Some claim it is a spoon with a bowl at each end (one a teaspoon, the other a tablespoon), centrally hinged so the spoon can be folded in half. Others assert that it is a long curved spork-like pickling spoon with three prongs.

## SOME WEDDING CAKE SYMBOLISM

A host of traditions surround the wedding cake: the newly wedded couple often make the first incision jointly holding the knife (a paradoxical act since a cut then binds them together); white icing is symbolic of purity and virginity; small pieces of cake are given to guests (and even sent to absent friends) to celebrate the union; the top tier of cake is often set aside and kept for the christening; some have suggested that each tier has a special symbolic meaning (compatibility, loyalty, fecundity, etc.); and the superstitious claim that a single woman who sleeps with a slice of wedding cake placed under her pillow will dream of her future spouse.

## CRÈMES DE ...

| | | | |
|---|---|---|---|
| *Crème d'abricots* | apricot | *Crème de fraises* | strawberry |
| *Crème d'amandes* | almond | *Crème de menthe* | peppermint |
| *Crème d'ananas* | pineapple | *Crème de moka* | coffee |
| *Crème de banane* | banana | *Crème de noyaux* | pips (almonds) |
| *Crème de cacao* | chocolate | *Crème de rose* | rose petal |
| *Crème de cassis* | blackcurrant | *Crème de vanille* | vanilla |
| *Crème de cerise* | cherry | *Crème de violette* | violet |

# SOME CALORIFIC VALUES

With a small 'c', a calorie is the amount of energy required to heat 1g of water by 1ºC. Calorie, with a capital 'C', is really a kilocalorie: 1,000 calories, the amount of energy required to heat 1kg of water by 1ºC, or 4.2kJ. Below are some approximate Calorie values for a range of foods calculated in portions of 100g or 100ml – although Calorie-counters should be aware that considerable variation often exists between sources:

| | | | |
|---|---|---|---|
| Apples | 47 | Lettuce, raw | 12 |
| Asparagus | 26 | Lobster, boiled | 120 |
| Avocado | 190 | Mangoes, raw | 55 |
| Bacon, fried | 450 | Mayonnaise | 700 |
| Banana | 95 | Meringue | 380 |
| Beans, baked | 75 | Milk, whole | 66 |
| Beef, roast | 210 | Mussels, boiled | 80 |
| Biscuits, chocolate | 530 | Oranges | 37 |
| Black pudding, fried | 300 | Parsnips, boiled | 66 |
| Broccoli, boiled | 25 | Partridge, roast | 215 |
| Butter | 740 | Paw-paw, raw | 35 |
| Cabbage, boiled | 15 | Pigeon, roast | 230 |
| Cake, sponge | 460 | Pilchards | 130 |
| Celery, raw | 7 | Plaice, poached | 95 |
| Cheese, Cheddar | 412 | Poppadoms, fried | 370 |
| Cherries, raw | 48 | Potatoes, roast | 150 |
| Chicken, roast | 150 | Raisins | 270 |
| Chocolate, milk | 530 | Rhubarb, unsweetened | 10 |
| Chocolate, plain | 525 | Rice, white | 140 |
| Christmas pudding | 330 | Salmon, smoked | 140 |
| Cola | 39 | Sausage, pork, grilled | 320 |
| Cola, diet | 0·25 | Saveloy | 260 |
| Corn flakes | 360 | Sesame seeds | 600 |
| Cream, double | 450 | Soy sauce | 70 |
| Cream, single | 200 | Spaghetti, boiled | 105 |
| Crisps | 550 | Spring onions, raw | 23 |
| Egg, boiled | 147 | Syrup, golden | 300 |
| Egg, fried | 180 | Tomato ketchup | 100 |
| Faggots | 270 | Tomatoes, raw | 17 |
| Goose, roast | 320 | Tripe, dressed | 65 |
| Grapes, raw | 60 | Turkey, roast | 150 |
| Grouse, roast | 175 | Venison, roast | 200 |
| Haggis, boiled | 310 | Walnuts | 690 |
| Hazelnuts | 650 | Whelks, boiled | 15 |
| Honey | 290 | Yoghurt, plain | 80 |
| Lard | 890 | Yorkshire pudding | 210 |

## EPICUREAN EPONYMS

FRANGIPANI · *almond-flavoured cream or pastry* · possibly created by the C16th Italian Marquis Muzio Frangipani, who invented a perfume to scent gloves.

SALLY LUNN· *sweetened teacake* · said to have been created by Sally Lunn, a Bath pastry chef (*c.*?1730).

THE SANDWICH · *slices of bread surrounding a filling* · a common item which became assocated with John Montagu, 4th Earl of Sandwich (1718–92), who ordered the snack to facilitate simultaneous eating and gambling.

APPLE CHARLOTTE · *layered apple cake* · created by Marc-Antoine Carême and (possibly) named in honour of Queen Charlotte (1744–1818), the consort of George III.

PAVLOVA· *meringue cake with fruit and cream* · probably created in New Zealand (Australians tend to disagree) in honour of the ballerina Anna Pavlova (1881–1931).

SAVARIN · *rum-laced fruit sponge* · named for writer Jean-Anthelme Brillat-Savarin (1755–1826).

BEEF WELLINGTON · *fillet steak in puff pastry* · named to honour the Duke of Wellington (1769–1852).

MOZART KUGELN · *marzipan and nougat cream, dipped in chocolate* · created in Vienna in 1890 by Salzburg confectioner Paul Furst, and named in honour of Mozart.

CARPACCIO · *extremely thin slices of raw beef garnished with oil, cheese, mustard, lemon juice or mayonnaise* · created by Giuseppe Cipriani, the founder of Harry's Bar in Venice. Like Melba toast, carpaccio was created to ameliorate a diet – this time, that of the Contessa Amalia Nani Mocenigo, who was forbidden to eat cooked meat. It was apparently inspired by the Renaissance painter Vittore Carpaccio (?1460–1525), known for his use of vibrant red pigment.

EARL GREY · *China tea infused with bergamot oil* · favoured by the 2nd Earl Grey (1764–1845).

NICOTINE· *an alkaloid present in tobacco leaves* · named after (and by) Jacques Nicot, a French diplomat based in Lisbon (*c.*1560) who popularised the cultivation of tobacco in France. (Nicot created his own eponym when compiling an early French dictionary.)

BÉCHAMEL SAUCE · *white sauce from flour, butter, and boiled milk, and infused with vegetables and seasonings* · created by and named after the French financier Marquis Louis de Béchamel (*d.*1703), a steward to Louis XIV.

MAYONNAISE · *thick sauce of egg yolks with oil, vinegar and seasoning* · named after the Minorcan port of Mahon, which in turn was named after the Carthaginian general Mago (*d.*203BC), who fought during Hannibal's Italian campaign.

## ——— EPICUREAN EPONYMS ———

GARIBALDI BISCUIT · *'squashed-fly biscuits'* · said to be named after Giuseppe Garibaldi (1807–82), the Italian Nationalist, who is said to have had a penchant for them.

EGGS BENEDICT · *a muffin (or toast) topped with grilled bacon and a poached egg, coated with Hollandaise sauce and garnished with a slice of truffle* · debate surrounds the invention and naming of the dish: a number of Benedicts are in the frame. However, a likely contender is the financier Lemuel Benedict, who apparently ordered it at the Waldorf Hotel (*c.*1894).

MADELEINE · *light sponge cake* · associated with the C19th French pastry chef Madeleine Paulmier.

SACHERTORTE · *rich, dry, rum-infused chocolate cake* · invented in Vienna by Franz Sacher (*c.*1832).

PEACH MELBA · *ice-cream served with peaches, and raspberry sauce* · named after soprano Dame Nellie Melba, by Georges Auguste Escoffier. (See Melba toast, p.11.)

TOM COLLINS · *iced cocktail of gin, lime (or lemon) juice, sugar and soda water* · possibly named after a C19th London bartender.

CHATEAUBRIAND · *a thick steak of beef cut from the middle of a fillet* · named after the French writer and diplomat Vicomte François-René de Chateaubriand (1768–1848). The steak was probably popularised at the French embassy in London by Chateaubriand's cook Montmirel.

LADY GREY · *blended tea with orange & lemon peel, and bergamot oil* · named after Lady Grey.

SALMONELLA · *a bacteria which causes food-poisoning in humans* · named after the American vet Daniel Elmer Salmon (1850–1914), who was the first to identify it.

LOGANBERRY · *the sweet purple berry of the raspberry plant* Rubus loganobaccus · created by the American judge and experimental horticulturalist James Harvey Logan, who developed the plant (*c.*1881). Some forty years later the botanist Rudolph Boysen created the hybrid BOYSENBERRY from the loganberry, the raspberry, and the blackberry.

GREENGAGES · *the green plum-like fruit of* Prunus insititia · named after the botanist Sir William Gage, who imported them from France (*c.*1725).

## ——— PHILLIP II ON FISH ———

Phillip II of Spain, the Consort of Queen Mary, is reported to have justified his dislike of fish with the following declaration: *They are nothing but element congealed, or a jelly of water.*

## LORD CHESTERFIELD ON CARVING

*Have you learned to carve well? For it is ridiculous not to carve well ... do you use yourself to carve adroitly and genteelly, without hacking half an hour across a bone, without bespattering the company with the sauce, and without over-turning the glasses into your neighbour's pocket?*

## THE PASSOVER MEAL

The Passover (or Pesach) meal is one of the most important in the Jewish calendar – commemorating the persecution of the Jews in Egypt, and celebrating their liberation from slavery. Much of the food and drink consumed during the Passover ceremony has some religious symbolism:

MATZAH · unleavened bread – symbolic of the swift flight of the Jews from Egypt when they had no time to wait for their dough to rise. (All leavened food, *hametz,* is prohibited during Passover.)

BETZA · a roasted egg – symbolic of the sacrificial offering of a roasted animal to God.

WINE · four cups of wine are drunk during the ceremony – possibly symbolic of the 'four promises of redemption', or the 'four empires of repression'. (An additional cup of wine is poured and left for the Prophet Elijah.)

KARPAS · green vegetables such as parsley or lettuce – symbolic of new growth. These are dipped in SALT WATER, which symbolises the tears of the slaves.

MAROR · bitter herbs, often chicory or horseradish – symbolic of the bitter toils of slavery.

HAROSET · a mixture of fruits and nuts with wine – symbolic of the mortar the slaves used to build the Pharaohs' pyramids.

ZEROAH · the shank-bone of a lamb – symbolic of the sacrificial paschal offering.

## UPPER CRUST

'Upper crust' has been long been slang for the aristocracy – the phrase derives from the tradition of baking bread in large (often communal) ovens. The poor received their bread from the lowest parts of the oven, which caused it to be charred by the coals, whereas the rich literally had the upper crust. Wynkyn de Worde's *The Booke of Kervinge* (1508) directs us to 'take a lofe in your lyfte hande, and pare ye lofe rounde about; then cut the ouer-cruste to your souerayne'. Where the lower bread touches the upper was known as the 'kissing-crust' – or *baisure de pain* in French.

## FOIE GRAS LIMERICK

There was an old gourmand of Crediton
Who ate pâté de foie gras having spread it on
A chocolate biscuit
He boomed 'Hell, I'll risk it!'
His tomb bears the date that he said it on.

## SCOVILLE SCALE

In 1912 Wilbur Scoville developed his now famous method to chart the comparative heat of different chillis (*J. Am. Pharm. Assoc.* 1912; 1:453–4). At the time of his research technologies such as microspectroscopy were not even dreamt of and Scoville had to rely on subjective tests of taste:

> *The method I have used is as follows: One grain of ground capsicum is macceated over night in 100 cc. of alcohol. After thorough shaking, filtered. This alcoholic solution is then added to sweetened water in definite proportions until a distinct but weak pungency is perceptible on the tongue.*

In this way, different chillis were progressively diluted until they could no longer be sensed on the tongue. The stronger the chilli, the more dilution required. Many considered such physiological tests to be controversial – Scoville even stated that they were 'tabooed in some quarters'. But, until chemical compositions could be analysed objectively, Scoville's physiological test offered 'a ready and satisfactory means of selecting capsicum' for medicinal and commercial purposes. From this test came the now famous Scoville Unit, which charted comparative chilli heats:

| Pepper | Scoville Units (SU) |
| --- | --- |
| Bell Pepper | 0 |
| Peperocini, Cherry Pepper | 100–500 |
| New Mexico, Aji Panca | 500–1,000 |
| Ancho, Passila, Espanola | 1,000–1,500 |
| Sandia, Rocotillo, Cascabel, Poblano | 1,500–2,500 |
| Jalapeno, Mirasol | 2,500–5,000 |
| Chilcostle, Louisiana Hot | 5,000–10,000 |
| de Arbol, Serrano, Japones | 10,000–30,000 |
| Piquin, Aji, Cayenne, Tabasco | 30,000–50,000 |
| Chiltepin, Tepin | 50,000–80,000 |
| Habanero, Scotch Bonnet | 80,000–300,000 |
| Pure Capsaicin | 16,000,000 |

*This can only be a rough guide, since the heat of chillis can vary from pepper to pepper.*

## DICKENS ON OYSTERS

*...the poorer a place is the greater call there seems for oysters. Look here, Sir, here's a oyster stall to every half dozen houses – the street's lined with 'em. Blessed if I don't think that when a man's very poor, he rushes out of his lodgings and eats oysters in regular desperation.*

— CHARLES DICKENS, *The Pickwick Papers*, 1836

## OLIVE OIL SPECIFICATION

Virgin olive oil is obtained from olives alone through purely mechanical (i.e. non-chemical) processes. Other than washing and filtering, the oil will not have gone through any other treatments, nor will it have been mixed with any other products. The International Olive Oil Council (IOOC) categorises virgin olive oil into the following four subdivisions:

EXTRA VIRGIN ....... first-class taste and aroma; oleic acid content <1%
VIRGIN .............. excellent taste and aroma; oleic acid content <2%
ORDINARY VIRGIN..... good taste and aroma; oleic acid content <3·3%
LAMPANTE ............ used for refining only; oleic acid content >3·3%

The United States Department of Agriculture (USDA) defines olive oil as:

*...the edible oil obtained from the fruit of the olive tree
(Olea europaea L.); is clarified, has a specific gravity of 0·910 to 0·915 at
25ºC; has an iodine number (Hanus) of 79 to 90;
has a refractive index of 1·4668 to 1·4683 at 25ºC...*

The USDA subdivides American olive oil into the following four grades:

US GRADE A *or* US FANCY · US GRADE B *or* US CHOICE
US GRADE C *or* US STANDARD · US GRADE D *or* US SUB-STANDARD

## CHURCHILL'S CREED

On discovering that his dining companion, the Arab leader Ibn Saud, forwent smoking and alcohol on religious grounds, Churchill retorted:

*I must point out that my rule of life prescribed as an
absolutely sacred rite smoking cigars and also the
drinking of alcohol before, after, and if need be
during all meals and in the intervals between them.*

## ——— MARTINIS &c. ———

It seems that gin was first created (*c.*1650) by Dr Franz de la Boë, who combined grain alcohol with juniper-oil to treat kidney disorders. Vermouth (white wine distilled with spices and herbs) derives from the German for wormwood, *Wermut*, and used to be employed as a treatment for intestinal worms. Combined, these spirits create the Martini, the cocktail which H.L. Mencken hailed as 'the only American invention as perfect as a sonnet'. The proportions of the Martini have always been controversial. Ernest Hemingway favoured the Montgomery: 15 gin to 1 vermouth (the odds Monty apparently gave on the battlefield). Richard Nixon – not as dry in any sense – opted for 7 gin to 1 vermouth. But Luis Buñuel considered it enough to hold up a glass of gin next to a bottle of vermouth and let a beam of sunlight pass through. Other mixes include:

| COCKTAIL | Vermouth Rosso | Dry Vermouth | Extra Dry Vermouth | Whiskey | Gin | Vodka | Angostura (dashes) | Orange bitters (drops) | Lime cordial | Soda water | GARNISH |
|---|---|---|---|---|---|---|---|---|---|---|---|
| Classic dry Martini | | ½ | | | 3 | | | | | | *olive* |
| Dry Martini | | ½ | | | 2½ | | 4 | | | | *olive* |
| Gimlet | | 2 | | | | | | | 1½ | | *wedge of lime* |
| Vodka Martini | | | ⅓ | | | 2 | | | | | *olive* |
| Gibson | | ½ | | | 3 | | | | | | *cocktail onion* |
| Manhattan | 2 | | | 1 | | | | | | | *cocktail cherry* |
| Bikini | 1 | | | | | 1 | | | | 3 | *orange peel* |
| Montgomery | | | 1 | | 15 | | | | | | |
| FDR | | 1 | | | 2 | | | | | | *olive* |
| Pink Martini | | 1 | | | 3 | 2 | | | | | |
| Vesper | | | | | 3 | 1 | | | | | *a dash of Lillet* |

*All equipment and each ingredient must be chilled before use.*

### SHAKEN OR STIRRED

Martinis should be agitated with ice before being drained into a cocktail glass. But how? Few questions have so vexed drinkers as whether to shake or stir a Martini. Shaking creates a colder drink than stirring, but it risks diluting the ingredients by prolonging their exposure to ice. Of course this dilemma is the fault of Ian Fleming's famous creation, James Bond, who added insult to uncertainty by eschewing gin in favour of vodka. To counter the confusion caused by Bond, we turn to Somerset Maugham:

> *A Martini should always be stirred, not shaken, so that*
> *the molecules lie sensuously on top of one another.*

## ——LUNCHEON VOUCHER DENOMINATIONS——

Devised in 1954 by John Hack, Luncheon Vouchers are exchangeable for meals, but not for cash, and are available in the following denominations:

15p · 25p · 30p · 50p · 75p · £1 · £1·50 · £2

## —————POTATOES & COOKING METHODS—————

| variety | origin | season | baking | boiling | chipping | mashing | roasting | salads |
|---|---|---|:---:|:---:|:---:|:---:|:---:|:---:|
| CARA | Ireland, 1976 | *maincrop late* | ☆ | ☆ | | | | |
| CHARLOTTE | France, 1981 | *maincrop* | ☆ | ☆ | | | | ☆ |
| DESIREE | Netherlands, 1962 | *maincrop* | ☆ | ☆ | ☆ | ☆ | ☆ | ☆ |
| ESTIMA | Netherlands, 1972 | *second early* | ☆ | ☆ | ☆ | | ☆ | |
| KING EDWARD | United Kingdom, 1902 | *maincrop* | ☆ | | ☆ | ☆ | ☆ | |
| MARFONA | Netherlands, 1977 | *second early* | ☆ | ☆ | ☆ | ☆ | | |
| MARIS PEER | United Kingdom, 1964 | *second early* | | ☆ | ☆ | | | ☆ |
| MARIS PIPER | United Kingdom, 1966 | *maincrop early* | ☆ | ☆ | ☆ | ☆ | ☆ | |
| NICOLA | West Germany, 1973 | *maincrop* | ☆ | ☆ | ☆ | ☆ | ☆ | ☆ |
| ROMANO | Netherlands, 1978 | *maincrop early* | ☆ | ☆ | | | ☆ | ☆ |
| SANTE | Netherlands, 1981 | *maincrop early* | ☆ | ☆ | ☆ | | ☆ | |
| WILJA | Netherlands, 1975 | *second early* | ☆ | ☆ | ☆ | ☆ | | |

## ——————'BAPTIZING' WINE——————

All – or nearly all – Red wine is the better for having just one or two drops of water poured into the *first* glass only. Why this should be I know not, but so it is. It introduces it. This admirable and little known custom is called 'Baptizing' wine.

— HILAIRE BELLOC, *Advice, c.*1950

## —————— MITHRIDATIZATION ——————

Mithridatization is the practice of protecting oneself against a poison by gradually self-administering non-lethal amounts. The word derives from Mithridates VI (*c.*163–132BC), the King of Pontus, who so feared being poisoned that he regularly ingested small doses in the hope of developing immunity. Having been defeated by Pompey, Mithridates attempted to kill himself with poison – but his mithridatization proved too successful, and he was instead compelled to order a mercenary to stab him to death.

———————— FINAL MEAL REQUESTS ————————

Since the death penalty was reinstated in the mid-1970s, Texas has had the dubious honour of executing more people than any other American State. The lethal injection Texas employs consists of sodium thiopental, pancuronium bromide, and potassium chloride (at a cost of $86·08). Below are the final meal requests from some of those executed in Texas.

JEFFERY DOUGHTIE
*executed on* 16.08.2001
8 soft fried eggs (wants yellow runny), big bowl of grits, 5 biscuits with bowl of butter, five pieces of fried hard and crisp bacon, two sausage patties, pitcher of chocolate milk, 2 pints vanilla Blue Bell ice cream, and 2 bananas

WILLIAM LITTLE
*executed on* 01.06.1999
15 slices of cheese, 3 fried eggs, 3 buttered toasts, 2 hamburger patties with cheese, 2 tomatoes sliced, 1 sliced onion, french fries with salad dressing, 2 lb. of crispy fried bacon, 1 quart chocolate milk and 1 pint of fresh strawberries

GERALD MITCHELL
*executed on* 22.10.2001
1 bag of assorted Jolly Ranchers

JOHNNY GARRETT
*executed on* 11.02.1992
Ice cream

SPENCER GOODMAN
*executed on* 18.01.2000
Double cheeseburger, french fries topped with onions and cheese, baked potato topped with sour cream, cheese and butter, 2 fried pork chops, 3 beef enchiladas, and chocolate cake

RONALD O'BRYAN
*executed on* 31.03.1984
T-bone steak (med. to well done), french fries & catsup, whole kernel corn, sweet peas, lettuce & tomato salad with egg & french dressing, iced tea, sweetener, saltines, Boston cream pie, rolls

*(The Texas Department of Criminal Justice is at pains to note that 'The final meal requested may not reflect the actual final meal served'.)*

The writer Grimod de la Reynière observed that during the French Revolution condemned prisoners were also focused on their last meals:

*the victims in the prisons are still preoccupied with food, and through the prison door pass some of the most exquisite dishes … in the bottom of the dungeons one finds those condemned ones making deals with restaurateurs, signing away one valuable after another…*

It has been claimed that President Françoise Mitterrand's very last meal included the illegal French delicacy ortolan, for details of which see p.128.

--------- SOME FOOD & DRINK TOPONYMS ---------

Amontillado [Montilla, Spain] . sherry
Angostura [Venezuela] ....... bitters
Arbroath [Scotland] ......... smokies
Atholl [Perthshire, Scotland] ..... brose
Bakewell [Derbyshire] ............ tart
Banbury [Oxfordshire] .......... cake
Bath ................... Oliver; bun
Battenberg [Germany] .......... cake
Béarnaise [Béarn, France] ....... sauce
Black Forest [Germany] ...... gâteau
Bourguignon [Burgundy] ....... beef
Brighton ...................... rock
Brussels [Belgium] .......... sprouts
Cayenne [French Guinea] ..... pepper
Chantilly [France] ............ cream
Cornish ...................... pasty
Cumberland ............... sausage
Danish ................... pastries
Demerara [Guyana] ........... sugar
Dijon [France] ............. mustard
Dover ....................... sole
Dundee ...................... cake
Eccles ...................... cake
Edinburgh ................... rock
Frankfurter ................ sausage
Genoa ...................... cake
Hollandaise ................ sauce
Irish ................. stew; coffee
Jerusalem[†] .............. artichoke

Kiev [Ukraine] ............. chicken
Lancashire ................. hotpot
Madeira ...................... cake
Maryland [USA] ........... chicken
Mayonnaise .... [Port Mahon, Minorca]
Neopolitan [Italy] ........ ice-cream
Nice [France] .............. biscuit
Ogen [Ha-Ogen kibbutz, Israel] .. melon
Pontefract [W. Yorkshire] ........ cake
Parma [Italy] .................... ham
Savoy [France] ............. cabbage
Seltzer [Nieder-Selters, Germany] . water
Seville [Spain] ............... orange
Singapore .................... Sling
Spanish ......... onion; omelette
Tabasco [E. Mexico] ............ sauce
Tangerine ........ [Tangiers, Morocco]
Tequila ................... [Mexico]
Vichy [France] ............. water
Welsh ..................... rarebit
Wiener [Vienna] .......... schnitzel
Worcestershire .............. sauce
Yorkshire ................. pudding

† Jerusalem artichokes do not come from Jerusalem and are not artichokes. The name is a corruption of *girasole* – the Italian for sunflower – which it resembles. Jerusalem artichokes *(Helianthis tuberosus)* actually originated in North America.

--------- COLONEL SANDERS ---------

Kentucky Fried Chicken's founder Colonel Harland Sanders (1890–1980) was a man of many (often hyphenated) jobs: farm-worker, street-car conductor, soldier, rail-road fireman, lawyer, insurance salesman, steam-boat ferryman, tyre salesman, service-station operator, and cook. Sanders perfected his 'secret-blend' of eleven herbs and spices at a service station in Corbin, Kentucky in the 1930s, and in 1964 he sold his six-hundred strong KFC franchise for $2m. Sanders's title was not military (he was only ever a private), rather it was from the Honorable Order of Kentucky Colonels[†], bestowed upon him in 1935 by the Governor, Ruby Laffoon.
† *Amongst the many famous Kentucky Colonels is Pope John Paul II, commissioned in 1965.*

## READING TEA LEAVES

Tasseography – the art of divination by means of reading tea leaves – has been traced back to 229BC, and the folk-tale of a Chinese princess who turned to her tea leaves, having been let down by astrology. There are many techniques for divining the secrets of the leaves, one of which is:

### PREPARATION

When the contents of the (plain white) cup have been drunk, save for a small residue of fluid (a teaspoonful or so), the drinker should agitate the cup to loosen the leaves[†]. The cup should then be inverted, placed upon its saucer, and rotated three times. The tasseographer can then take the cup for interpretation, ensuring the handle points towards the subject.

### INTERPRETATION

A quantity of leaves bulked together signifies wealth and prosperity. A single leaf at the rim of the cup is highly auspicious, as are human forms. Leaves on the sides of the cup signify that change will be quick; those at the bottom of the cup that change will be laborious. Wavy lines signify trouble or woe; straight lines signify peace. In interpreting specific shapes, or 'hieroglyphs', the larger the image the more significant its meaning. Dots around any image magnify its importance, as do lines leading to it. Below, a few hieroglyphs are deciphered, and some shapes are explained.

| leaves | starfish | lobster | fish |
|--------|----------|---------|------|
| *change* | *good luck* | *security* | *uncertainty* |

| *Shape* | *Meaning* | | |
|---------|-----------|---|---|
| Bird | *good news from home* | Dog | *fidelity* |
| Cat | *jealousy* | Flower | *friendship* |
| Seagull | *news from afar* | Bell | *joy* |
| Wheel | *new employment* | Lifebuoy | *safety at sea* |
| Sword | *disagreements* | Serpent | *treachery* |
| Triangle | *painful loss* | Sheaf | *prosperity* |
| Tree | *temptation* | Bed | *sickness* |
| Star | *good fortune* | Heart | *good news from afar* |
| Circle | *a wedding* | Axe | *division, separation* |
| Airship | *great danger* | Dragon | *false fears* |
| | | Hammer | *auspicious new start* |

† *It is perhaps superfluous to note that tea from tea-bags is of absolutely no use whatsoever.*

## 'CHIPS' CHANNON'S PARTIES

Sir Henry 'Chips' Channon (1897–1958) was a socialite, businessman, and MP celebrated for his indiscreet and fascinating diaries. Channon's social circle was extensive, spanning politics, celebrity, and royalty, and his houses in Essex and Belgrave Square were the location of many society parties. Channon had an unusual technique for ensuring the success of his parties. The following is from his diary entry for 25 November 1947:

> *My own big dinner, and as usual the house 'played up' and looked very grand and glittering, lit up and full of yellow chrysanthe-mums from Kelvedon. I 'laced' the cocktails with Benzedrine, which I find always makes a party go. Noël Coward arrived first, wearing what he called the 'Coward emeralds', and everyone was in gala dress – white ties and the women dripping with jewels.*

## TO SHARPEN A CARVING KNIFE

## BEN & JERRY'S ICE-CREAM FLAVOURS

Created in 1978 by Ben Cohen and Jerry Greenfield, Ben & Jerry's ice-creams became famed both for their quality and for their curious names:

| | |
|---|---|
| Karamel Sutra | Vanilla Caramel Fudge |
| Berry N'Ice | The Full VerMonty |
| Phish Food[†] | Chocolate Fudge Brownie |
| Chunky Monkey | One Sweet Whirled |
| New York Super Fudge Chunk | Caramel Chew Chew |
| Cookie Dough | Cherry Garcia[§] |
| Half Baked | Honey, I'm Home! |

[†]A mix of fudge, marshmallow nougat, caramel, and ice-cream named after the Vermont-based, genre-defying rock-band Phish. § Cherry Garcia (cherry-flavoured ice-cream with extra cherries and dark-chocolate chunks) is named in honour of Jerry Garcia – guitarist, song-writer, and co-founder of the legendary American rock-group The Grateful Dead.

## GEORGE WASHINGTON'S RULES

As a youth, George Washington kept a commonplace book entitled *Forms of Writing*. Amongst other miscellaneous items this book contained 110 *'Rules of Civility and Decent Behaviour in Company and Conversation'*. Many writers have discussed the possible source of these maxims and it seems likely that they originate from the work of sixteenth century French Jesuits. A few of the Rules which relate to food, drink, and the etiquette of entertaining are quoted, as Moncure Conway puts it, 'with the hope that they will do more than amuse the reader by their quaintness'.

90th · Being Sat at meat Scratch not neither Spit Cough or blow your Nose except there's a Necessity for it.

92nd · Take no Salt or cut Bread with your Knife Greasy.

93rd · Entertaining any one at table it is decent to present him wt. meat, Undertake not to help others undesired by ye. Master.

94th · If you Soak bread in the Sauce let it be no more than what you put in your Mouth at a time and blow not your broth at Table but Stay till Cools of it Self.

95th · Put not your meat to your Mouth with your Knife in your hand neither Spit forth the Stones of any fruit Pye upon a dish not cast anything under the table

96th · It's unbecoming to Stoop to one's Meat. Keep your Fingers clean & when foul wipe them in a Corner of your Table Napkin.

97th · Put not another bite into your Mouth till the former be swallowed let not your Morsels be too big for the jowls.

98th · Drink to nor talk with your mouth full neither Gaze about you while you are a Drinking.

99th · Drink not too leisurely nor yet too hastily. Before and after Drinking wipe your Lips, breathe not then or Ever with too Great a Noise, for it is uncivil.

100th · Cleanse not your teeth with the Table Cloth Napkin Fork or Knife but if others do let it be done wt. a Pick Tooth.

101st · Rinse not your Mouth in the Presence of Others.

102nd · It is out of use to call upon the Company often to Eat, nor need you Drink to others every Time you Drink.

103rd · In Company of your Betters be not [longer in eating] that they are lay not your Arm but ar[rise] with only a touch on the edge of the table.

---

*Unfortunately, the exact wording of a few of Washington's Rules has been lost to history as a result of damage to the original manuscript by mice.*

—————————— BETTING BOOK ENTRIES ——————————

Every evening during term-time the Fellows of Gonville & Caius College, Cambridge, gather for dinner in Hall, after which they may adjourn to the Combination Room for a dessert of wine and fruit. By a tradition that dates back to 1789 any wagers made during dessert are recorded in the Betting Book – which is also used to record any social 'fines' (paid in wine), as well as wine presented to commemorate a special occasion:

Mr Hanmer bets Mr Pemberton one bottle of port that Mr Hanmer's hair will not be cut during the next twelve months.

(23 iii 1789) *Lost by Mr Hanmer and paid*

Mr Brinkley bets Mr Davy one bottle of port that Mr Davy is not 5'10" high without his shoes.

(21 vi 1790) *Lost by Mr Davy*

Mr Holden offers to give one bottle of port if the English should take 6 ships of the line from the French in the year 1794. (4 vi 1794)

Mr Borton promises a bottle of port when peace is proclaimed between England and France.

*Paid by Mr Borton April 30 1802*

Mr Caplin bets Mr Hemming that he hops 300 yards in 300 or less hops. (6 vi 1794) *Lost by Mr Caplin*

Mr Barton bets Mr Grigby one bottle of port that Mr Pitt will not be minister of this country when peace is concluded with the French Republic. (25 xii 1796) *Lost by Mr Grigby*

Mr Jones bets Mr Lucas one bottle of port that in the course of months, Bank Notes will be universally a legal tender throughout Great Britain. (26 iv 1797) *Lost by Mr Jones*

Mr Wright bets Mr Barton 5 bottles of wine that the income tax is not repealed either this or the next session of Parliament. (30 iii 1802)

The President presents the room with 6 bottles of wine to commemorate the glorious victory [The Battle of Trafalgar] obtained over the combined fleets of France and Spain on the 21st of October 1805 by Lord Nelson. (21 x 1805)

*(The other fellows presented 44 additional bottles.)*

Mr Chapman bets Mr Lucas that Mr Lucas cannot ascend six rungs of a ladder by his arms alone.

(10 xii 1807) *Lost by Mr Chapman*

Mr Chad was fined by the House for making a frivolous and vexatious motion. (4 iii 1808)

To celebrate the glorious Victories of the Allies over Buonaparte near Leipzig on the 15th, 18th & 19th of October 1813. (5 xi 1813) *15 bottles*

Mr White bets the President that his (Mr W's) saddle is twice as old as the President's newest saddle.

(21 v 1816) *Lost by Mr White*

Mr Norgate bets Mr Okes that it is not allowable for any man to marry his wife's father's sister. (12 xi 1817)

—————— BETTING BOOK ENTRIES cont. ——————

To celebrate the aerial voyage of Dr Woodehouse in a Balloon from Cambridge to Brancher (?) Park.

(15 v 1830) *18 bottles presented*

Whoever has today's *Times* is fined a bottle of wine.

(4 xii 1856) *Found in the Master's Lodge*

Mr Davy bets Mr Garrick that 'hare-brained' is so spelt in Johnson's Dictionary. (28 xi 1870)

Mr Caldwell bets Dr Guillemard that at the present moment there are not 700 lepers in Bergen. (1886)

Professor Wood bets Mr Stratton that a new planet outside Neptune will be discovered before women get the suffrage.(3 i 1909) *Lost by Prof Wood*

Captain Leslie bets Mr Casey that England will be at peace within 12 calendar months. (27 viii 1914)

Dr Chappel bets Mr Barnes that the Chinese were in a position to see objects the size of the order of 7μ, before 1550 AD. (3 ii 1964)

Dr Goodhart bets Mr Tranchell that King John is reported to have died of a surfeit of Lampreys.

(11 iii 1964) *Lost by Dr Goodhart*

Mr Barnes bets Dr Goodhart that it can be proved that he, Dr Goodhart, is not at the centre of the universe. (17 iii 1964)

*Lost by Mr Barnes; settled by Dr Stephen Hawking*

Dr Abulafia, inadvertently having struck Dr Casey in the eye while explaining the fundamental basis of Einstein's General Theory of Relativity, undertakes to recompense the Society, in order to express his apology. (10 i 1977)

Dr Casey bets Dr Buck that in the Southern hemisphere the port circulates anti-clockwise.

(24 viii 1979) *Won by Dr Casey*

Dr Edwards presents wine to the room in order to mark the fact that Prof. Hawking is presiding. And Dr Whaley presents wine to mark the first time that Grace was said by a machine. (22 ix 1987)

—————— YE OLDE CHESHIRE CHEESE ——————

Ye Olde Cheshire Cheese is a public house in Wine Office Court, Fleet Street, London. It has stood (in one form or other) since the C16th, and has been patronised by Dickens, Johnson, Twain, Beerbohm, Yates, and Chesterton, amongst many others. The Cheese has long been famed for its huge meat pies (weighing up to 80lb) – and for a parrot called Polly, whose death in 1926, at the age of forty, resulted in numerous newspaper obituaries. The Cheese used to employ idiosyncratic codewords to order spirits: Gin was always called for as RACK, Scotch whisky was simply SCOTCH (it wasn't done to say whisky), and Irish whiskey was just CORK.

## — COELIAC DISEASE & GLUTEN INTOLERANCE —

Coeliac disease is a chronic condition that causes the inner surface of the small intestine to be damaged by gluten (a protein found in wheat, rye, barley, and oats) thereby hampering the digestion and absorption of food. Although the cause of coeliac disease remains uncertain, a link with the immune system has been suggested. As many as 1 in 300 might be affected by the disease, the symptoms of which can include diarrhoea, weight loss, lethargy, anaemia, and depression. For most sufferers the only treatment is adherence to a strict gluten-free diet. This is by no means a simple task, since gluten may occur in a host of foodstuffs, including breads, cakes, biscuits and pasta. Additionally, sufferers must check the ingredients of processed foods, condiments, and even a few medications.

## — TINNED FOOD —

Techniques for canning food developed during the C19th, but have their basis in bottling and sealing, which have been practised throughout the ages. In 1938 two cans of food (one veal; one carrots) which had survived an 1824 Arctic expedition were opened for investigation. Samples of the food were chemically analysed (additionally the veal was fed to rats and cats) and both were discovered to be sound and – theoretically – safe to eat. Yet food in cans has always attracted a degree of opprobrium, as John Carey discusses in *The Intellectuals and the Masses*, 1992. Carey notes that a host of writers (including E.M. Forster, T.S. Eliot, Graham Greene, and John Betjeman) used tinned food as a shorthand for the proletariat:

> *In the intellectual's conceptual vocabulary tinned food ... offends against what the intellectual designates as nature: it is mechanical and soulless.*

Indeed, George Orwell claimed that WWI could never have occurred if tinned food had not been invented. Orwell wrote: 'We may find in the long run that tinned food is a deadlier weapon than the machine gun.' Prime Minister Harold Wilson, as if proving Carey's point, said in 1962:

> *If I had the choice between smoked salmon and tinned salmon, I'd have it tinned. With vinegar.*

## — NIGELLA'S BITE —

Nigella seeds *(Nigella sativa)* are used as a condiment in Indian cuisine to flavour breads like naan. Their peppery flavour gives them a slight bite.

## —COCA-COLA LOGOS—

Coca-Cola was registered as a trademark in 1887, and since then it has become one of the most recognised images on Earth. Below are some of the Coca-Cola logos employed in different locations around the world:

[Somalia]

[Egypt]

[Israel]

[Thailand]

[France]

[Japan]

[Sri Lanka · Sinhalese]

[Taiwan]

[Morocco]

[Korea]

[China]

[Bulgaria]

[Russia]

[Pakistan]

[Ethiopia]

*'Coca-Cola' and 'Coke' are registered trade marks of the Coca-Cola Company and are reproduced with kind permission from the Coca-Cola Company.*

—————————————— SPACE FOOD ——————————————

Dining in space presents a range of practical and culinary challenges, from ensuring adequate nutrition, to dealing with food in zero gravity. Because weight and space are limited, food on NASA's shuttle missions is limited to 3·8lb per person per day (including 1lb packaging). NASA categorises the food it carries on missions into the following six groups:

REHYDRATABLE . . . . . . . . . . . . . . . . . . . . . *soups, macaroni cheese, scrambled eggs*
THERMOSTABILIZED . . . . . . . . . . . . . . . . . . *fruits, tuna, salmon, chicken, beef*
INTERMEDIATE MOISTURE . . . . . . . . . . . . . . . . . . *dried peaches and apricots*
NATURAL FORM . . . . . . . . . . . . . . . . . . . . . . . . . . . . . *nuts, cereal bars, biscuits*
IRRADIATED MEAT . . . . . . . . . . . . . *beef (for storage at ambient temperature)*
CONDIMENTS . . . . . . . . . . . . . . . . . . . . . . . . . . . . *ketchup, mustard, pepper sauce*
(To counteract microgravity, salt is dissolved in water, and pepper suspended in oil.)

NASA astronauts select their own menus from a 'Baseline Shuttle Food List' up to five months before takeoff and their choices are analysed by the Shuttle Dietitian to ensure they form a healthy and balanced diet. Independent of the normal supplies is the Safe Haven Food – 22 days' worth of ambient-temperature food designed to provide a minimum of 2,000 Calories per person per day in case of an on-board system failure.

—————————————— HUMBLE PIE ——————————————

Although 'eating humble pie' is the proverbial method of demonstrating contrition or abasement, it is perfectly possible to prepare and consume the dish. 'Humbles' (or 'numbles') refers to venison offal – probably deriving from the old French term for deer entrails, *nombles*. Robert May in his 1660 book *The Accomplisht Cook* demonstrates a simple pie recipe:

> TO MAKE UMBLE-PIE · *Lay minced beef-suet in the bottom of the pie, or slices of interlarded bacon, and the umbles cut as big as small dices, with some bacon cut in the same form, and seasoned with nutmeg, pepper, and salt. Fill your pies with it, and slices of bacon and butter, close it up and bake it, and liquor it with claret, butter and stripped thyme.*

—————————————— CHOCOLATE MONEY ——————————————

Trade amongst the Nahau was primarily by barter, although nibs (grains) of cacao were sometimes used as money. These nibs, known as *patlachté*, were widely accepted – the largest unit being 8,000 nibs or a *xiquipilli*.

## ─── TASTES LIKE… ───

| *Flesh of…* | *is said to taste like* |
| --- | --- |
| Tapir[1] | beef |
| Puma[1] | veal |
| Water hare | tapir |
| Hippopotamus[2] | beef |
| Armadillo | rabbit |
| Wombat | pork |
| Baby wasps[3] | scrambled egg |
| Porcupine | sucking pig; fowl |
| Bat | partridge |
| Lion | veal |
| Swan[4] | fishy game |
| Fox | rabbit |
| Iguana[5] | capon; rabbit |
| Beaver | pork |
| Bear | between beef and pork |
| Horse | beef |
| Kangaroo | venison |
| Giant waterbug[6] | Gorgonzola |
| Nephila spider[6] | potato |
| Walrus | game |
| Badger | mutton |
| Durian[7] | chestnuts |
| Flying-fox | game |
| Sea slug[8] | green fat of turtle |
| Termites | lettuce |
| Flamingo | fishy wild-duck |
| Crocodile[9] | pork; lobster |
| Boa-constrictor[10] | veal |
| Dog | pork; lamb; goat |
| Monkey[11] | rabbit |
| Reindeer | game; beef |

These descriptions have been taken from a variety of sources – including personal and anecdotal experience – though a valuable text was Peter Lund Simmonds's superb 1859 account *The Curiosities of Food*. [1] According to Charles Darwin in his *Journal of a Naturalist*. [2] Portuguese settlers in Africa were permitted to eat hippopotamus meat during Lent. This was based on the somewhat tendentious ecclesiastical logic that since hippos spent so much time in the water, they could technically be classified as fish. [3] Pascal Khoo Thwe, a member of the Burmese Padaung, notes the taste of baby wasps is 'somewhere between scrambled-egg and roasted prawn, depending on how mature they are'. [4] See also the entry on swans on p.146. [5] Osbert Sitwell claims capon; others claim rabbit. [6] From the records of W.S. Bristowe. [7] Alexandre Dumas make this comparison (see p.78). [8] Mr Wingrave Cooke. [9] The Revd Mr Hansel in *Letters on the Nicobar Islands* claims pork; whereas Dr Madden in *Travels in Egypt* claims lobster. [10] Mr Buckland in *Curiosities of Natural History*. [11] Mr Wallace in *Travels on the Amazon*.

## ─── EVELYN WAUGH ON CORKED WINE ───

*I have heard people complain their wine was 'corked' when they found a fragment of broken cork floating in the glass. When wine is truly corky the cork is diseased and foul smelling, and the wine is more or less tainted. It should never be drunk in this condition … it is for this reason that a small quantity of wine is invariably poured first into the host's glass for him to taste … If the host is so barbarous as to taste and accept a corky wine, all that the guest can do is to refrain from drinking it and never come to that table again.*

— EVELYN WAUGH, *Wine in Peace and War*, 1949

## COCKTAILS

### – BACHELOR'S –
DREAM

½ <sup>C</sup>uraçao
½ <sup>M</sup>araschino
¼ Crême <sup>V</sup>iolet
*Stir together, and
strain into a cocktail
glass. Garnish with
fresh whipped cream.*

### – CLASSIC –
DAIQUIRI
*Shake 2 rum with the
juice of 1 lime, and a
teaspoonful of sugar.
Garnish with a
twist of lemon.*

### – HOT PORT –
NEGUS
*Fill a tall glass ⅔ full
of hot water. Add ½ a
sugar lump & 3 ruby
port. Stir, & dust with
grated nutmeg.*

### – B52 –

2 <sup>K</sup>aluah · 2 <sup>B</sup>aileys
2 <sup>G</sup>rand Marnier
*Gently pour the spirits
into a tumbler.*

### – MINT JULEP –
*Put in a tumbler 2½
tablespoons water, 1
tablespoon sugar, and
3 sprigs fresh mint.
Press the mint well to
release its flavour, and
add 2½ glasses
bourbon. Fill glass
with crushed ice,
garnish with sugar.*

### – RUSTY NAIL –

1 ½ <sup>S</sup>cotch whisky
¾ <sup>D</sup>rambuie
*Stir and pour over ice.*

### – ADONIS –

1½ <sup>D</sup>ry sherry
¾ <sup>S</sup>weet vermouth
*Add a dash of orange
bitters, stir, pour over
ice, and garnish with
an orange twist.*

### – ABSINTHE –
COCKTAIL
*Add 1 dash of
Angostura bitters and
1 dash of Anisette to
¾ Absinthe & shake.*

### – COSMOPOLITAN –

1½ <sup>V</sup>odka
1 <sup>C</sup>ointreau
1½ Cranberry <sup>J</sup>uice
¼ <sup>L</sup>ime juice
*Shake well together,
strain and garnish
with an orange twist.*

### – MARGARITA –

2 <sup>T</sup>equila
1 Triple <sup>S</sup>ec
2 <sup>L</sup>ime juice
*Shake with ice &
strain into a salted
glass, add lime wedge.*

### – SINGAPORE –
SLING

¼ dry <sup>G</sup>in
½ <sup>C</sup>herry brandy
*Add juice of ¼ lime,
shake, & strain over
ice into a tall glass,
top up with soda.*

## COCKTAILS

### – THE SIDECAR –

1½ ᶜognac
¾ Cointreaᵁ
¾ ᴸemon juice
*Shake together, strain over ice into a sugared cocktail glass, garnish with a twist of lemon.*

### – CHAMPAGNE –
### COCKTAIL

*Drop a cube of sugar in a flute. Dash with Angostura bitters, top up with chilled champagne, & garnish with orange peel .*

### – LONG ISLAND –
### ICE TEA

¼ ᵀriple Sec · ¾ ᴳin
¾ ᵂhite rum
¾ ⱽodka
¾ ᵀᴱquila · ½ a lime
¾ ᴼrange juice, cola.
*Squeeze the lime into a tall glass with ice. Add the spirits, stir, and fill with cola.*

### – BLOODY MARY –

*Mix tomato juice with Worcestershire sauce, celery salt, ground pepper, and a dash (or three) of Tabasco. Pour this combination over ice and 2 vodka. Some like to add a dash of fino (dry) sherry, and others add fresh horse-radish for extra bite.*

### – NEGRONI –

1½ ᴳin
1½ ˢweet vermouth
1½ ᶜampari
*Shake spirits and pour over ice into a tall glass. Top up the glass with iced soda water, and garnish with the peel of an orange.*

### – MOJITO –

*Place a handful of fresh mint leaves into a tall glass and add 1 tsp. of sugar syrup. Mash the mint and syrup with vigour. Add the juice of ½ a lime & 2 white rum. Fill with soda water, & garnish with mint.*

### – SEABREEZE –

2 ⱽodka
2 ᶜranberry juice
1 ᴳrapefruit juice
*Shake, and strain over ice into a tall glass.*

### – WHISKY SOUR –

*Add a teaspoon of sugar and the juice of ½ a lemon to 1 rye (or bourbon). Shake, & pour into a tumbler.*

### – KAMIKAZE –

2 ⱽodka
½ ᵀriple Sec
*Add a teaspoonful of lime juice, shake with ice and strain.*

### – BELLINI –

*Sieve the pulp of fresh white peaches. Mix 3 parts juice to 1 part dry champagne or Prosecco. (Some also add a dash of brandy.) Serve chilled.*

Measures are in fl.oz ≈ 25ml. There are a number of variations for many of these mixes.

---
## BLACK VELVET
---

Black velvet – the mixture of champagne and Guinness – was invented in 1861 at the London gentleman's club Brooks's. Legend has it that as a mark of respect after the death of Albert, the Prince Consort, the club's barman put the champagne into mourning by adding a slug of Guinness. This concoction grew popular, and was apparently the favourite drink of the 'Iron Chancellor' Otto von Bismarck, although many others have condemned black velvet as the flagrant contamination of two fine drinks.

*To make black velvet: mix champagne and Guinness in equal measures,*
*adding the latter to the former to avoid excessive effervescence.*

---
## DINING TIMES FOR MONKS
---

Taken from *The Rule of St Benedict, c.AD535*

CAPUT XLI · *Quibus horis oporteat reficere Fratres*
(CHAPTER XLI · At what hours are the Brethren to take their meals)

From Holy Easter until Pentecost let the brethren dine at the sixth hour, and sup in the evening. But from Pentecost throughout the summer (unless they have work to do in the fields, or are harassed by excessive heat) let them fast on Wednesdays and Fridays until the ninth hour, but on other days dine at the sixth. Should they have field labour, or should the heat of the summer be very great, they must always take their dinner at the sixth hour. Let the Abbot provide for this, and let him so arrange and dispose all things, that souls may be saved, and that the brethren may do what they have to do without just cause for murmuring. From the fourteenth of September until the beginning of Lent let them always dine at the ninth hour; and during Lent, until Easter, in the evening. And let the hour of the evening meal be so ordered that they have no need of a lamp while eating, but let all be over while it is yet daylight. At all times, whether of dinner or supper, let the hour be so arranged that everything be done by daylight.

---
## PEPYS ON TEE
---

*... we talked together of the interest of this kingdom to have a peace with*
*Spain and a war with France and Holland ... And afterwards did send for*
*a Cupp of Tee (a China drink) of which I never had before, and went away.'*

— SAMUEL PEPYS, *Diary*, 25 September 1660

## ——APHRODISIACS & ANTI-APHRODISIACS——

For centuries men and women have searched for aphrodisiacs and, as John Davenport wrote in his 1859 essay *Aphrodisiacs & Anti-Aphrodisiacs,*

> *...the vegetable, animal, and mineral kingdoms have been ransacked for the purpose of discovering remedies capable for strengthening the genital apparatus, and exciting it to action.*

Notable of mention are: orchids (*orchis* is the Greek word for testicle); whirtleberries; snowdrops; partridge brains (mashed into powder and swallowed with red wine); and truffles (which were so prized by George IV that he instructed his ambassadors in Europe to dispatch any prize specimens to the royal kitchen by state messenger). Seafood is strongly represented in the roll-call of aphrodisiacs. The power of oysters was notorious even in Juvenal's time, but lobsters, crabs, sea hedgehogs, and cuttlefish have also had their advocates. The Romans appear to have embraced love potions with a passion: openly sold on the streets of Rome were concoctions such as frog's bones, sucking-fish, dried marrow, and nail-parings. Mushrooms were also favoured, prompting Martial's verse:

> *If envious age relax the nuptial knot,*
> *Thy food be mushrooms, and thy feast shallot.*

Although many have championed aphrodisiacs it does not follow that they have been universally welcomed. In the C17th certain orders of monks were forbidden to eat or drink chocolate for fear of its stimulating effects. Ancient Venetian law (Cap.XVI: *Dei maleficii et herbarie*) made the administration of love potions a serious criminal offence. Lady Grey was accused in Parliament of employing aphrodisiacs to bewitch Edward VI. Moreover, although it might appear that everything has, at some time, been classed an aphrodisiac, there are a number of items which 'may be efficaciously employed in moderating, or rather checking, too violent a propensity to venery'. Lettuce, cucumbers, endives, lemons, sorrel, camphor, and milk have all been considered anti-aphrodisiacs because of their cooling qualities. Should these prove insufficient, Plato and Aristotle both advised walking barefoot to check carnal desire. John Davenport recommends the study of mathematics ('in all ages, mathematicians have been but little disposed to love') – he goes on to point out what might seem obvious, that leprosy has an anti-aphrodisiac effect. According to Rabelais 'carnal concupiscence is cooled and quelled in five several ways':

> [1] by the means of *wine...*    [2] by certain *drugs...*
> [3] by frequent *labour* and continual *toiling...*    [4] by an eager *study...*
> [5] by the too frequent *reiteration* of the act of *venery...*

## —— AMBROSIA, NECTAR, AND MANNA ——

AMBROSIA is the fabled food of the gods which made them immortal; NECTAR is their fabled drink. MANNA is the food which miraculously appeared to the Israelites in the wilderness after their escape from Egypt.

## —— McDONALD'S GLOBAL PRESENCE ——

McDonald's has over 30,000 restaurants in 121 countries and territories:

American Samoa · Andorra · Argentina · Aruba · Australia · Austria
Azerbaijan · Bahamas · Bahrain · Belarus · Belgium · Bermuda · Bolivia
Brazil · Brunei · Bulgaria · Canada · Chile · China · Colombia
Costa Rica · Croatia · Cuba · Cyprus · Czech Republic · Denmark
Dominican Republic · Ecuador · Eire [which serves the Shamrock Shake
around St Patrick's Day]· Egypt · El Salvador · Estonia · Fiji
Finland [with the first McDonald's within the Arctic Circle, opened in 1997]
France · Georgia · Germany · Gibraltar · Greece · Guadeloupe · Guam
Guatemala · Guyana · Honduras · Hong Kong · Hungary [opened in
1998] Iceland · India [where the mutton Maharaja Mac is served] · Indonesia
Israel [all meat is Kosher, with 7 Kosher-only restaurants] · Italy · Jamaica
Japan [which serves the Teriyaki McBurger] · Jordan · Korea [which serves the
pork Bulgogi Burger] · Kuwait · Latvia · Lebanon · Liechtenstein
Lithuania · Luxembourg · Macau · Macedonia · Malaysia · Malta
Martinique · Mauritius · Mexico · Moldova · Monaco · Morocco
Netherland Antilles · Netherlands [which serves the special McKroket]
New Caledonia · New Zealand · Nicaragua · Norway · Oman · Pakistan
Panama · Paraguay · Peru · Philippines · Poland · Portugal · Puerto Rico
Qatar · Reunion Island · Romania · Russia [the Pushkin Square McDonald's is
the world's busiest] · St Maarten · Saipan · San Marino · Saudi Arabia
Singapore · Slovakia · Slovenia · S. Africa · Sri Lanka · Spain · Suriname
Sweden · Switzerland [which serves the Swiss Vegi Mac] · Tahiti · Taiwan
Thailand · Trinidad · Turkey · Ukraine · United Arab Emirates · UK
USA · Uruguay · Venezuela · Virgin Islands · W. Samoa · Yugoslavia

## —— SOME NOTABLE 19TH-CENTURY CHEFS ——

| | | | |
|---|---|---|---|
| Hopwood ... *employed by* Lord Foley | Bonny ........ Duke of Buccleuch |
| Ude................. Earl of Sefton | Brûnet......... Duke of Montrose |
| Moret........... Royal Household | Halinger..... Baron de Rothschild |
| Aberlin ...... Duke of Devonshire | Frottier....... Duke of Cambridge |
| Chaudeau.. Marq. of Landsdowne | Douetil........ Duke of Cleveland |
| Crépin..... Duchess of Sutherland | Perron..... Marq. of Londonderry |

---------------------- CAPTAIN BIRDSEYE ----------------------

While working as a fur-trader in Labrador during the 1910s, Clarence Birdseye (1886–1956) observed how effectively food was preserved by the Arctic climate. As a child Birdseye had been interested both in taxidermy and cookery, and he quickly saw the potential of freezing as a means by which food might be stored. Back in America, Birdseye experimented with freezing techniques and discovered that fast-freezing produced small ice-crystals which left the structure (and taste) of food relatively intact. In 1924 he founded the company which was later to become General Foods. Although Birdseye did work with the US Army, it is not clear whether he was actually a captain – indeed, some sources describe him as a colonel.

---------------------- CHÂTEAU MOUTON ROTHSCHILD LABELS ----------------------

In 1924 Baron Philippe de Rothschild changed the face of wine bottles by commissioning the celebrated poster designer Jean Carlu to create a new label for that year's vintage. Twenty-one years later, at the Liberation, a 'V for Victory' design by Philippe Jullian was placed on the labels and an annual tradition was born. Since 1945, a stellar cast of artists has been commissioned to decorate the labels of Mouton Rothschild, including:

| | | | |
|---|---|---|---|
| 1947 | Jean Cocteau | 1973 | Pablo Picasso |
| 1955 | Georges Braque | 1974 | Robert Motherwell |
| 1958 | Salvador Dali | 1975 | Andy Warhol |
| 1964 | Henry Moore | 1988 | Keith Haring |
| 1969 | Joan Miró | 1993 | Balthus† |
| 1971 | Wassily Kandinsky | 1999 | Raymond Savignac |

† The label designed by Balthus (Balthazar Kossowski de Rola) was a line drawing of a reclining, naked young girl. The label was initially approved by the American Bureau of Alcohol, Tobacco and Firearms (BATF), whose jurisdiction extends to the design and wording on US wine labels. However, after complaints from a Californian pressure group ('The Sexual Assault Response Team') Mouton Rothschild asked the BATF to rescind its approval of the label, and the US market was supplied with bottles featuring a blank space where the Balthus image had been. (Balthus's original bottles are now highly prized.)

---------------------- THE OSLO BREAKFAST ----------------------

Norway's *Oslo Breakfast* was an attempt in 1929 to improve the health of schoolchildren, who were given the following free meal each morning:

½ pint milk · wholemeal bread · cheese · ½ orange · ½ apple
a dose of cod-liver oil (September–March)

## A FEW GREEK FOOD TERMS

| | | | |
|---|---|---|---|
| Avgolemono | *... egg and lemon soup* | Psomi | *....... bread* |
| Baklava | *..... filo pastry, nuts, honey* | Psari | *........ fish* |
| Bourekakia | *.......... feta filo puffs* | Rigani | *....... oregano* |
| Dolmades | *....... stuffed vine leaves* | Rizogalo | *. rice pudding & cinnamon* |
| Feta | *............. white goat's cheese* | Skordalia | *............ garlic spread* |
| Gouvetsi | *............ lamb casserole* | Souvlakia | *......... skewered kebabs* |
| Horta | *. dandelions with oil & lemon* | Spanakopeta | *....... spinach filo pie* |
| Kalamarakia | *.................. squid* | Tahini | *...... sesame-seed paste/soup* |
| Kourabiedes | *....... sugared biscuits* | Taramosalata | *........ fish roe spread* |
| Mezethes | *........ savoury appetisers* | Tiropita | *.......... cheese-stuffed filo* |
| Mousaka | *.. aubergine, meat casserole* | Tsatziki | *. cucumber, yogurt, garlic dip* |
| Karpouzi | *.............. watermelon* | Xifias | *..................... swordfish* |

## BAKED ALASKA

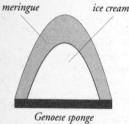

*meringue*     *ice cream*

*Genoese sponge*
*(soaked in liqueur)*

Part dessert, part physics experiment, Baked Alaska has an uncertain history. One explanation is that the unlikely notion of cooking ice-cream with meringue was developed by a chef at the Hôtel de Paris – possibly Giroux or Balzac. Yet some credit Count Rumford with inventing the idea; others credit Charles Ranhofer; and those that are left credit an unnamed chef from China who visited France in 1867 as part of a Chinese delegation. The secret of the pudding is that the air trapped inside the meringue insulates the ice-cream from the heat of the oven whilst the meringue (and the sponge base upon which it sits) is browned. Baked Alaska can appear under the names: *Norwegian Omelette, Omelette Soufflée Surprise, Omelette Norvégienne, Omelette Suédoise, Peña Santa,* and *Alaska Florida.*

## BOXTY

An Irish form of potato bread, boxty (*bacstaí* in Irish) is made from flour, mashed potato, and raw potato. The dish is traditionally made on New Year's Day and Halloween, and it inspired the following Irish folk-rhyme:

> *Boxty on the griddle, boxty in the pan,*
> *If you can't make boxty, you'll never get a man!*

———————————— SWIFT'S WIND ————————————

A curious pamphlet published pseudonymously in London in 1722 gives a pun-packed account of the benefits to women of flatulence; it is almost certainly the work of Jonathan Swift (1667–1745). The title page reads:

The benefit of FARTING explained
or the
FUNDAMENT-ALL cause of the distempers incident to the *Fair Sex*,
inquir'd into, Proving a *Posteriori* most of the disorders *In-tail'd* upon
them, are owing to *Flatulencies* not seasonably vented.

———————

Wrote in *Spanish* by Don *Fartinando Puff-indorst*
Professor of *Bumbast* in the University of *Craccow*
AND
Translated into *English* at the Request and for the Use of the
Lady *Damp-fart* of *Her-fart-shire*
BY
*Obadiah Fizle*, Groom of the Stool to
the Princess of *Arsimini* in *Sardinia*

———————

[Printed by Simon Bumbubbard, at the Sign of the Wind-Mill]

Fartinando Puff-indorst (i.e. Swift) first provides his definition of a fart:

*A Nitro-aerial Vapour, exhal'd from an adjacent pond
of Stagnant Water of a Saline Nature, and rarefied and
Sublim'd into the Nose of a Microcosmical Alembic, by
the gentle heat of a Stercorarios Balneum, with a
strong Empyreuma, and forced through the Posteriours
by the compressive power of the expulsive Faculty.*

His argument is then threefold: first, that women suffer 'ill consequences' from suppressing flatulence; second, that farting breaks neither Canon Law nor the Laws of Nature ('*tho' it seems to be against the Civil Law*'); and third, that '*many advantages will attend an Act of Tolerance*'. These advantages include allowing women the liberty to eat '*peas-porridge*' and drink '*bottled cyder*' – as well as promoting mirth in the general company.

———————————— STORING CIGARS ————————————

The optimum location for storing cigars is in a humidor maintained at:

TEMPERATURE: 65–70ºF *or* 18–21ºC · HUMIDITY: 65–70%

# OFFAL

Offal (from the Old English 'off fall', and the German *Abfall*, meaning rubbish) is the edible waste of a butchered animal. Traditionally, offal applied only to entrails, but its use has been widened to include any other animal parts (brains, tongues, tails, feet) which can be sold as food. In America offal is known as 'organ meat' or 'variety meats' – the latter term indicative of a general squeamishness surrounding such body parts which has prompted the development of a glossary of euphemistic offal terms:

| | | | |
|---|---|---|---|
| Heart, liver, lungs | *pluck* | Spleen | *melts* |
| Offal from birds | *gibblets* | Pigs' intestines | *chitterlings* |
| Lungs | *lights* | Venison offal (see p.60) | *(h)umbles* |

Perhaps because offal is cheap and widely available most cultures enjoy dishes which employ these uncommercial cuts of meat. The French *ferchuse* combines pig hearts and lights with red wine, potatoes, and onions; British *faggots* are pork offal with breadcumbs, onions, and flavourings wrapped in intestines[†]; the Italian *quaggiaridda* is a mixture of lamb offal with cheese wrapped in a pig's caul and baked; *jitrnice* is a Czech sausage of liver and lungs; and the Scottish national dish, *haggis*, is made with the minced heart, liver, and lungs of a sheep encased in a sheep's stomach (see p.36). Because offal spoils relatively quickly, it needs to be cooked soon after slaughter. As a consequence it is often to be found in dishes such as *brawn* (meat jelly), pâté, sausages, or *haslet* (meat-loaf).

[†] It is claimed that the 1666 Great Fire of London started when a batch of faggots caught fire at a shop in Pudding Lane. The fire destroyed 13,200 dwellings, 87 parish churches, as well as St Paul's and other public buildings, but killed fewer than 20.

# WINE BARREL SIZES

Nowadays wine is fermented, matured, and stored in a host of materials from concrete to stainless steel. Traditionally, wooden barrels were employed – and a complex nomenclature of barrel specifications existed:

| *Name* | *Litres* | | |
|---|---|---|---|
| | | Demi-muid (Châteauneuf-du-Pape) | 600 |
| | | Fuder (Mosel) | 1,000 |
| Barrique bordelaise (Bordeaux) | 225 | Stück (Rhine) | 1,200 |
| Tonneau (Bordeaux) | 900 | Halbstück (Rhine) | 600 |
| Pièce (Burgundy) | 228 | Barricas bordelesas (Spain) | 225 |
| Feuillette (Chablis) | 132 | Caratelli (Vin Santo, Italy) | varies |
| Cognac barrel | 350 | Quartaut | 57 |
| Champagne barrel | 205 | Gönci (Tokaji, Hungary) | 136 |

## FAVISM

Favism is a relatively uncommon disease triggered by consumption of or contact with fava beans *(Vicia faba)*. Favism is a genetic condition (more prevalent in males) that affects those who are deficient in the glucose-6-phosphate dehydrogenase enzyme found in red blood cells. The effect of favism is to destroy these blood cells, causing acute anaemia. Famously, Pythagoras urged his followers to abstain from beans *('A fabis abstinete!')* though it is unclear whether or not he was aware of the risks of favism.

## BRITISH PUB SIGNS & PUB CRICKET

The etymology of many pub names is obvious, deriving from: brewing *(The Grapes; The Bottle & Basket)*; hunting *(The Hare & Hounds)*; specific professions *(The Good Doctor; The Printer's Devil)*; loyalty to the monarch *(The Crown, The King's Head)*; the countryside *(The Wheatsheaf)*, and so on. However, other names have more curious and complex derivations:

Albion.................................... *the ancient name for England*
Alma............................ *the first battle of the Crimean War (1854)*
Bag O'Nails .................................... *? corruption of Bacchanals*
Beetle & Wedge....... *a beetle is the hammer used to drive wooden wedges*
Black Lion .......................... *from the arms of Phillipa of Hainault*
Blue Boar................................ *emblem of the Earl of Oxford*
Cat & Fiddle ........... *? corruption of La Chatte Fidèle (the faithful cat)*
Crossed Keys....... *the keys of the Kingdom of Heaven, emblem of St Peter*
Elephant & Castle ..... *? corruption of Infanta de Castil – Edward I's wife*
Falcon........................................ *emblem of Elizabeth I*
Feathers ...................................... *? emblem of the Prince of Wales*
Green Man ...... *Jack o' the Green, Celtic god of fertility; also, Robin Hood*
Intrepid Fox ................. *the politician Charles James Fox (1749–1806)*
Lamb & Flag ........................ *represents Christ and His resurrection*
Marquis of Granby .............................. *John Manners (1721–70)*
Mother Shipton........... *a Yorkshire-born psychic and witch (1488–?1560)*
Pelican .............................. *symbolic of Christ and charity*
Punchbowl........... *symbolic of the Whig party (the Tories drank claret)*
Red Lion ................................ *emblem of John of Gaunt*
Royal Oak .. *symbol of Charles II's escape after the Battle of Worcester (1651)*
Talbot.......... *a breed of hunting dog – emblem of the Earl of Shrewsbury*
Tuns............... *a large wood barrel – emblem of the Vintners' Company*

The game of 'pub cricket' was devised to while away the hours of a long car drive. Each player takes an innings in turn and scores one run for every leg (animal or human) depicted on the pub signs which are passed. Players are 'caught out' if they miss a sign spotted by another player, or 'bowled out' if they pass a sign which has no legs depicted.

## ──── DANGEROUS FOOD AND DRINK ────

KING JOHN (1167–1216) · it is commonly stated that King John died from a 'surfeit of LAMPREYS' but it is more likely that he died from dysentery. In *King John* William Shakespeare has the King poisoned: 'Within me is a hell; and there the poison is, as a fiend, confined to tyrannize On unreprievable condemned blood.'

GABRIELLE D'ESTRÉES (1573–99) · Mistress of Henry IV of France, who died from eating an ORANGE.

GEORGE, DUKE OF CLARENCE (1449–78) · secretly executed in the Tower of London by his brother, King Edward IV. It is commonly claimed that George was either drowned in a vat of MALMSEY wine, or that his body was dumped there later. Shakespeare alludes to this story in *King Richard III* when the Duke of Clarence's murderer declares while stabbing him: 'Take that, and that: if all this will not do, I'll drown you in the malmsey-butt within.'

FRANCIS BACON (1561–1626) · died of pneumonia caught while stuffing a CHICKEN with snow as part of an experiment into cold.

ANACREON (*c.*570–485BC) · Greek lyric poet who choked to death on a GRAPE-STONE.

THOMAS OTWAY (1652–85) · poet and dramatist famed for two plays *The Orphan* (1680) and *Venice Preserv'd* (1682). Reduced to penury Otway was given a guinea by a well-wisher. He purchased a loaf of BREAD, but choked to death on the first mouthful.

TYCHO BRAHE (1546–1601) · legend has it that the Danish astronomer died from a distended bladder, after drinking a surfeit of WINE while dining with the Baron of Rosenberg. It seems that Brahe was far too preoccupied about contravening social etiquette to rise from the dinner table.

GEORGE W. BUSH · 43rd President of the United States who, on 13 January 2002, at 5.35pm, lost consciousness for a few seconds after choking on a PRETZEL.

QUINTUS FABIUS MAXIMUS (*fl.*200BC) · the Roman praetor who choked to death on a single goat-hair within a cup of MILK.

COLMAN ITADACH · the 'Thirsty Monk' who, in strict observance of the Rule of St Patrick, refused to drink any water whilst working in the fields and died of THIRST.

[See: Vatel, p.101; Fugu, p.138; & Poisonous Mushrooms, p.142.]

## ──── UBUKASHYA ────

The Bemba people of Zambia call their craving for meat *Ubukashya*.

## ──────── CORONATION & JUBILEE CHICKEN ────────

*Coronation Chicken* was created in 1953 for the Coronation of Queen Elizabeth II by Constance Spry and Rosemary Hume. (At the time it was bestowed the curiously un-English name *Poulet Reine Elizabeth*.) The dish (cold chicken in a creamy curry sauce with a salad of rice, green peas, and herbs) was not actually served at the Coronation banquet, but at a later lunch for Commonwealth heads of state[†]. In 2002, to mark the Queen's Golden Jubilee, a competition was held amongst the royal chefs to create an updated version of this classic dish. The winner (chosen by the Queen) was head-chef Lionel Mann whose *Jubilee Chicken* is also served cold, but with crème fraîche, ginger, and lime, and accompanied by a pasta salad.

† The lunch menu for the Coronation banquet, served at Buckingham Palace, was:
  *Consommé Royale · Filet de Boeuf à la Mascotte · Salade · Glace à la Mangue*

## ──────────── GLUTTONY ────────────

> *Let it be said that of all the deadly sins that mankind may commit, the fifth appears to be the one that least troubles his conscience and causes him the least remorse.*

### — GRIMOD DE LA REYNIÈRE

Gluttony derives from the Latin verb *gluttire* – to gulp down or swallow. St Thomas Aquinas listed five ways by which one might commit the sin:

| | |
|---|---|
| *Praepropere* | by eating too soon |
| *Laute* | by eating too expensively |
| *Nimis* | by eating too much |
| *Ardenter* | by eating too eagerly |
| *Studiose* | by eating too daintily |

Aristotle wrote of Philoxenos, who longed to have the neck of a crane so that he might enjoy his food for longer before it entered his stomach.

## ──────────── THE IMAM FAINTED ────────────

The Turkish dish of aubergine stuffed with onions, garlic, and tomatoes and simmered in olive oil is known as *Imam Bayildi,* which translates as 'the Imam fainted'. Many stories exist to explain this curious name – from the Imam fainting because of the delightful aroma or taste of the dish, to his collapse on discovering the quantity and cost of the olive oil.

—————— CULINARY & HOUSEHOLD HINTS ——————

### To Remove Fruit Stains
Pour boiling water over stained surface, having it fall from a distance of three feet. This is a much better way than dipping stain in and out of hot water; or wring articles out of cold water and hang outside on a frosty night.

### To Scald Milk
Put in top of double boiler, having water boiling in under part. Cover, and let stand on top of range until milk around edge of double boiler has a beadlike appearance.

### To Remove Stains of Claret Wine
As soon as claret is spilt, cover spot with salt. Let stand a few minutes, then rinse in cold water. (See p.91.)

### To Chop Parsley
Remove leaves from parsley and dry with a towel if wet. Gather and compact the parsley between thumb and fingers. With a sharp vegetable knife cut through and through. Again gather in fingers and recut, so continuing until parsley is finely cut.

### To Wash Mirrors and Windows
Rub over with chamois skin wrung out of warm water, then wipe with a piece of dry chamois skin. This method saves much strength.

### To Thicken a Moustache
Take 1oz of tincture of cantharides, 1oz of tincture of capsicum, and 1oz of rosewater. Mix into a lotion, and rub well into the moustache *mane et nocte*.

### Removing the Odour of Cigars
Burn a little coffee in a metal container and carry it through where cigars have been smoked.

### To Clean White Ostrich Feathers
Four ounces of white soap, cut small and dissolve in four pints of warm water; beat the solution into a lather. Introduce the feathers and rub well by hand for 5–6 minutes. After which, wash them in clean water as hot as can be borne. Shake before the fire until dry.

### To Avoid Bad Odour
Milk and butter very quickly absorb odours, and if in a refrigerator with other foods, should be kept closely covered.

### To Deter Mice
Mice have a great dislike to the smell of peppermint; a little oil of peppermint placed round their haunts will keep the pests away.

### To Remove Iron Rust
Saturate spot with lemon juice, then cover with salt. Let stand in the sun for several hours; or a solution of hydrochloric acid may be used.

### Removing the Odour of Fish
A lemon rubbed over knives and forks will remove the odour of fish.

### To Extract Juice from Onion
Cut a slice from root end of onion, draw back the skin, and press onion on a coarse grater, working with a rotary motion.

──────── CULINARY & HOUSEHOLD HINTS cont. ────────

### Dying Gloves

White kid gloves may be dyed tan by dipping them in saffron water until they are the desired colour.

### To Caramelise Sugar

Put in a smooth granite saucepan or omelet pan, place over hot part of range, and stir constantly until melted and of the colour of maple syrup. Care must be taken to prevent sugar from adhering to sides of pan or spoon.

### To Clean Piano Keys

Rub the keys gently with alcohol.

### To Prevent Salt from Lumping

Mix with corn-starch, allowing one teaspoon corn-starch to six teaspoons salt.

### To Perfume Note-Paper

Take a few quires of blotting paper and sprinkle each sheet with the desired perfume. Weight the papers down until they are dry. Then, interleave writing paper and envelopes with the blotting paper and press the whole together for some hours. (The be-perfumed blotting paper may be reused several times.)

### In Sweeping Carpets

Keep broom close to floor and work with the grain of the carpet. Occasionally turn broom that it may wear evenly.

[The author has not tested and is unable to vouch for any of these remedies, many of which appear curious at the very least.]

──────── MIREPOIX ────────

Mirepoix is the combination of diced vegetables (usually celery, onion, carrot), and occasionally meat (bacon or ham), that is gently sautéed and used as a garnish or to impart flavour to sauces. It was probably named after the C18th French ambassador Charles de Lévis, duc de Mirepoix.

──────── GOVERNMENT DIETARY ADVICE ────────

The British Government specifies eight 'Guidelines for a Healthy Diet':

Enjoy your food.
Eat a variety of different foods.
Eat the right amount to be a healthy weight.
Eat plenty of foods rich in starch and fibre.
Eat plenty of fruit and vegetables.
Don't eat too many foods that contain a lot of fat.
Don't have sugary foods and drinks too often.
If you drink alcohol, drink sensibly.

---
## TOBLERONE PEAKS
---

Each size of the Swiss chocolate Toblerone has a specific number of peaks:

| Size | peaks | 50g | 11 | 200g | 15 |
|------|-------|------|----|------|----|
| mini | 3 | 75g | 11 | 400g | 15 |
| 35g | 9 | 100g (& 4.5kg) | 12 | 750g | 17 |

---
## SPITTING FOOD OUT
---

*The Management of Bones and Pits*

Terrapin bones, fish bones and grape seeds must be eaten quite bare and clean in the mouth, and removed one at a time between finger and thumb. All spitting out of bones and pits into the plate is disgusting. If food is too hot, quickly take a swallow of water. On no account spit it out! If food has been taken into your mouth, no matter how you hate it, you have got to swallow it. It is unforgivable to take anything out of your mouth that has been put in it, except dry bones, and stones. To spit anything whatever into the corner of your napkin, is too nauseating to comment on ... The only way to take anything out of your mouth is between first-finger and thumb. Dry grape seeds or cherry pits can be dropped from the lips into the cupped hand. Peaches or other very juicy fruits are peeled and then eaten with knife and fork, but dry fruits, such as apples, may be cut and then eaten in the fingers. Never wipe hands that have fruit juice on them on a napkin without first using a finger bowl, because fruit juices make indelible stains.

— EMILY POST, *Etiquette In Society*, 1922

---
## HONEYMOON
---

Samuel Johnson's *Dictionary* defined a honeymoon as: 'The first month after marriage, when there is nothing but tenderness and pleasure.' The *Oxford English Dictionary* states that the term relates to newly-wedded love which waxes and wanes like the changing moon. Others claim that the honeymoon derives from an ancient Teutonic tradition where newly-weds would drink hydromel (honey-wine, or metheglin) for thirty days after the marriage ceremony in the hope it would aid fertility. It is said that Attila the Hun (*c.*406–453) died from a nasal haemorrhage just after his marriage to Ildico due to overindulgence in metheglin at his wedding.

[Splendidly, honeymoon in German is *Flitterwochen* – roughly meaning *glittering weeks*.]

## —— SOME FRENCH COOKING DESCRIPTIONS ——

| DESCRIPTION | CHARACTERISTIC INGREDIENTS |
|---|---|
| À l'Africaine | aubergines, potatoes, cucumber, courgettes |
| À l'Algérienne | sweet potato-croquettes, tomatoes, garlic |
| À l'Alsacienne | sauerkraut, ham, bacon, Strasbourg sausage |
| À l'Anversoise | hop shoots in butter or cream |
| À la Basquaise | ham, ceps, potatoes |
| À la Beauharnais | artichokes, stuffed mushrooms, tarragon |
| À la Biarrotte | ceps, potato cakes |
| À la Boulangère | sliced potatoes, onions, stock, butter |
| À la Bourguignonne | wine, shallots, mushrooms, bacon |
| À la Brabanconne | Brussels sprouts, hops or chicory |
| À la Bretonne | haricot beans |
| À la Catalane | aubergine, tomatoes, rice (varies) |
| À la Châtelaine | artichoke hearts, chestnuts, puréed onions, cream |
| À la Chilienne | rice, red peppers |
| À la Conti | puréed lentils, bacon |
| À la Cussy | artichoke hearts, mushroom purée, truffle, kidneys |
| À la Du Barry | château potatoes, grated cheese, cauliflower Mornay |
| À la Favorite [roasts] | artichoke hearts, potatoes, celery |
| À la Favorite [steaks] | asparagus tips, pâté de foie gras, truffles |
| À la Fermière | carrots, onions, celery, turnips, (etc.), in butter |
| À la Forestière | mushrooms, ham or bacon, potatoes |
| À la Hongroise | paprika, onions, tomatoes, sour cream, (etc.) |
| À la Jardinière | spring vegetables: carrots, turnips, French beans, (etc.) |
| À la Landaise | Bayonne ham, mushrooms, goose fat |
| À la Languedocienne | ceps, aubergines, chopped tomatoes |
| À la Limousine | red cabbage, ceps, chestnuts |
| À la Lyonnaise | fried chopped onion, parsley |
| À la Maraîchère | carrots, onions, cucumber, artichoke hearts |
| À la Marocaine | courgettes, sweet peppers, saffron rice, tomatoes |
| À la Mascotte | artichoke hearts, truffles, potatoes |
| À la Niçoise | tomatoes, anchovies, French beans, garlic, potatoes, (etc.) |
| À l'Orientale | tomatoes stuffed with (saffron) pilaf rice, okara, peppers |
| À la Parisienne | potatoes, artichoke hearts, braised lettuce |
| À la Portugaise | dishes with a preponderance of tomatoes |
| À la Princesse | asparagus tips (sometimes with Béchamel sauce), truffle |
| À la Printanière | spring vegetables, butter |
| À la Romaine | spinach, tomato, potatoes, (etc.) |
| À la Sarde | rice, tomatoes, stuffed cucumber, mushrooms |
| À la Tivoli | asparagus tips, mushrooms, kidneys, suprême sauce |
| À la Tyrolienne | tomatoes, fried onions |
| À la Valenciennes | rice in meat stock, with sweet peppers, ham |
| À la Zingara | paprika, tomatoes, (varies) |

—————— FANNIE FARMER ON FLUIDS ——————

American cook Fannie Farmer (1857–1915), enumerated 7 uses of beverages:

*To quench thirst · To introduce water into the circulatory system*
*To regulate body temperature · To assist in carrying off waste*
*To stimulate the nervous system and various organs*
*To nourish · For medicinal purposes*

—————————— DURIAN ——————————

The tropical fruit Durian *(Durio zibethinus)* enjoys the rare distinction of being banned throughout the entire Singapore transport system – as well as from many hotels, airlines, and public buildings. The simple reason is that the large, oval, spiky fruit *(dury* is Malay for spike) smells very bad indeed. (Indeed, the odour of durian is so overpowering that many have noted that the smell pervades after tinning.) The chef Anthony Bourdain, with a characteristically vivid simile, wrote: 'It smelled like you'd buried somebody holding a big wheel of Stilton in his arms, then dug him up a few weeks later.' Yet it seems that the taste of durian more than makes up for its odour – to again quote Bourdain: 'Imagine a mix of Camembert cheese, avocado, and smoked Gouda. OK, don't. That's not a very good description … It didn't taste anything like it smelled; the flavour was much less assertive, and curiously addictive.' The fruit is eaten in a variety of ways: raw, in ice-cream, as a vegetable, in cakes, fried with onions, salt, and vinegar, roasted with coconut oil, or made into jams and sweets. Durian can weigh over 2kg and, since durian trees often reach heights of 30m, falling durian can be fatal – as Alfred Wallace noted in 1869:

> *When the fruit begins to ripen it falls daily and almost hourly, and accidents not unfrequently happen to persons walking or working under the trees. When a durian strikes a man in its fall, it produces a dreadful wound, the strong spines tearing open the flesh, while the blow itself is very heavy; but from this circumstance, death rarely ensues, the copious effusions of blood preventing the inflammation which might otherwise take place.*

—————————— TO WASH DECANTERS ——————————

Rinse the decanter with warm water, then half fill it with hot soapsuds and add one teaspoonful of washing soda. Insert shreds of newspaper torn in small pieces. Let stand for half an hour, occasionally shaking. Empty, rinse with hot water, drain, wipe the outside, and let stand to dry inside.

─────────── HALAL ───────────

*Halal* (also *hallal* and *halaal*) is Arabic for lawful or permitted, and is used to describe the food that conforms to Islamic dietary law. The opposite of *halal* is *haraam*, which means unlawful or prohibited. For foodstuffs which are questionable, the term *mashbooh* (uncertain) is used. Certain categories of animal are always considered *haraam*, including:

carrion · animals which have been strangled
animals killed by beating · animals killed by falling from a height
animals which have been killed by wild beasts
animals which have been gored on the horns of another animal
animals which have not been killed in the name of Allah
pork (and all its by-products) · mules and asses
carnivorous animals (wolves, lions, etc.) · birds of prey (eagles, etc.)

*Halal* animals include sheep, goats, cattle, poultry, rabbits, game, and so on, but only if they have been slaughtered according to *thabah* – methods approved by Islamic law. *Thabah* has a number of rules that are designed to minimise the suffering and ensure the dignity of animals before they die – some of which are common to traditional Jewish *kosher* methods:

animals should not be cruelly transported or handled
animals should be fed before slaughter
animals should not be blindfolded
animals should be killed by a Muslim in the name of Allah
animals should not be slaughtered in the presence of another animal
knives should not be sharpened in the presence of animals
animals should not be stunned before slaughter
animals should be slaughtered quickly and professionally

Further rules exist: to ensure religious respect; to prevent contamination; and to address the complexities surrounding such issues as medicinal alcohol, processed food, gelatin, cheese, whey, rennet, and E-numbers.

─────── EATING ESTABLISHMENTS IN FINLAND ───────

| | |
|---|---|
| Baari | a snack bar, usually unlicensed |
| Grilli | an informal restaurant, popular for lunches |
| Kahvila | café or snack bar serving cakes and pastries |
| Kahvio | self-service cafeteria |
| Krouvi | a small restaurant |
| Ravintola | a restaurant |
| Yökhero | a night club |

## RUNYON'S GREATEST RESTAURANTS

According to Damon Runyon, the greatest pre-WWI restaurants were:

Delmonico's *(New York)* · Voisin's *(Paris)* · Hotel Adlon *(Berlin)*
Wolter's *(Nancy)* · Savoy Hotel *(London)*

## –IVOROUS

| Term | Feeding on |
|---|---|
| Aurivorous[†] | gold |
| Baccivorous | berries |
| Canivorous | dogs |
| Carnivorous | meat, flesh, animals |
| Cepivorous | onions |
| [Cultrivorous | knife-swallowing] |
| Detritivorous | decaying matter |
| Equivorous | horse-flesh |
| Folivorous | leaves, foliage |
| Frondivorous | leaves |
| Fructivorous | fruit |
| Fucivorous | seaweed |
| Fumivorous | snake |
| Fungivorous | funghi |
| Galactophagous | milk |
| Gallinivorous | poultry |
| Graminivorous | grass, herbs |
| Granivorous | seeds, grain |
| Herbivorous | plants |
| Hominivorous | humans |
| Insectivorous | insects |
| Lactivorous | milk |
| Larvivorous | larvae |
| Leguminivorous | beans & peas |
| Lichenivorous | lichen |
| Lignivorous | wood |
| Mellivorous | honey |
| Merdivorous | dung |
| Nectarivorous | nectar |
| Nucivorous | nuts |
| Offivorous | offal |
| Omnivorous | everything |
| Ornithivorous | birds |
| Oryzivorous | rice |
| Ossivorous | bones |
| Ovivorous | eggs; sheep |
| Panivorous | bread |
| Phytivorous | plant matter |
| Pinivorous | pine kernels |
| Piperivorous | pepper |
| Piscivorous | fish |
| Pollinivorous | pollen |
| Pomivorous | apples |
| Quercivorous | oak leaves |
| Radicivorous | roots |
| Ranivorous | frogs |
| Reptilivorous | reptiles |
| Sanguivorous | blood |
| Seminivorous | seeds |
| Vermivorous | vermin, grubs |

[†]Horace Walpole wrote that
'Man is an aurivorous animal'.

## FRANK MUIR ON HEALTH FOOD

*Some breakfast food manufacturer hit upon the simple notion of emptying out the leavings of carthorse nosebags, adding a few other things like unconsumed portions of chicken layer's mash, and the sweepings of racing stables, packing the mixture in little bags and selling them in health food shops.*

———————————— SAKE ————————————

*Sake,* as well as a generic Japanese term for alcoholic drink, is wine made from fermented rice, known commonly in Japan as *seishu* or *nihonshu.* *Sake* was first brewed in Japan *c.*AD300 and since that time (despite the occasional law banning its manufacture and consumption) *sake* has become a central element of Japanese culture and cuisine. A vast array of *sake* is produced in Japan from the highest-quality *ginjoshu* to local varieties of *jizake,* and (illicit) home-brewed *doburoku.* In addition, *sake* is available sweet *(amakuchi),* dry *(karakuchi),* carbonated, or unrefined *(nigorizake)* – with a panoply of tastes to rival the varieties of grape wine. For some time there has been debate as to the temperature *sake* should be served. Traditionally, most *sake* was drunk warm – having been heated in an earthenware bottle *(tokkuri)* to around 50ºC (122ºF). But as quality improved, so it seems the fashion for enjoying chilled *sake* developed. At least for Western audiences, the temperature at which *sake* should be served has been immortalised by James Bond in *You Only Live Twice:*

> *'Do you like Japanese sake, Mr Bond?*
> *Or would you prefer Vodka Martini?'*
> Tiger Tanaka

> *'No, no, I like sake, especially when it is served at the correct*
> *temperature – 98·4 degrees Fahrenheit – like this is.'*
> James Bond

> *'For a European, you are exceptionally cultivated.'*
> Tiger Tanaka


————— TRIMALCHIO ON 'COSTIVENESS' —————

'Pardon me, my Friends,' said he [Trimalchio], 'I have been costive for several days, and my Physicians were to seek about it, when a Suppository of Pomegranate Wine, with the Liquor of a Pine-tree and Vinegar relieved me; and now I hope my belly may be ashamed if it keep to better Order; for otherwise I have such a rumbling in my Guts, you'd think an Ox bellowed … There's not one of us born without some defect or other, and I think no torment greater than wanting the benefit of going to stool, which is the only thing even Jupiter himself cannot prevent … believe me, this being hard-bound, if it gets into the Head disturbs the whole body; I have known many a Man lost by it, when they have been so modest to themselves as not to tell what they ailed.'

*Trimalchio's Feast* from the *Satyrica* of Petronius (*c.*AD66)

─────────── FOUR FRUITS ───────────

The following four fruits *(quatre-fruits)* are the traditional summer fruits combined together in France to make preserves, compotes, and syrups:

strawberries · redcurrants · cherries · raspberries

The four yellow fruits *(quatre-fruits jaunes)* used for the same purpose are:

lemons · citrons · oranges · Seville oranges

─────────── FROGS' LEGS ───────────

A number of recipes for frogs' legs exist. The Lebanese marinade their frogs' legs in olive oil suffused with salt, pepper, and garlic, re-using the marinade as a basting fluid while the legs are charcoal-grilled. A similar technique is popular in Spain, where butter is used for basting. However, the country most commonly associated with frogs' legs is France, where a number of variations are popular. A few of the more common recipes are:

*Grenouilles à la Meunière* · the legs are seasoned, floured and fried in butter, then garnished with lemon juice, parsley, and butter.

*Grenouilles à la Lyonnaise* · the legs are browned in hot butter with thinly sliced onions, and served with a parsley and vinegar sauce.

*Grenouilles à la Provencale*[†] · the legs are fried in olive oil before crushed garlic, chopped parsley, salt and pepper are added.

*Grenouilles à la Niçoise* · the legs are browned in butter before being sautéed with tomato, onion, garlic, tarragon, and pimento.

† The recipe preferred by Pope Pius IV (1499–1565) according to chef Bartolomeo Scappi.

─────────── SMARTIES COLOURS ───────────

In 1937 H.I. Rowntree & Co. launched *Chocolate Beans*, renaming them *Smarties* a year later. Since then nine colours of *Smarties* have been made:

*red · yellow · orange · green · mauve · pink · light-brown · brown · blue*

Orange *Smarties* are the most popular – perhaps because they are orange-flavoured. Prior to 1958 dark brown *Smarties* were filled with coffee chocolate and light-brown *Smarties* with plain chocolate. (Brown is the least popular colour.) Blue *Smarties* replaced light-brown ones in 1989.

———— HIPPOPHAGY or EATING HORSES ————

Perhaps because of a sentimental fondness for horses, or because of an inherited Roman distaste for the meat, the British have long had a strong aversion to hippophagy – eating horse-flesh. Yet, horses *(Equus caballus)* are eaten by numerous cultures across the world including in Belgium, Sweden, China, Japan, India, and South America. In France it was illegal to eat horse-flesh until 1811, when the testimony of many (including Napoleon's pharmacist) persuaded legislators to amend the law. It is possible that experiences during the Napoleonic War, when many survived by eating army horses, played a part in changing opinions – although after the ban was lifted, horse-meat banquets were staged for the public to prove how delicious was the flesh. On 1 December 1855, eleven VIPs (journalists, doctors, civil servants) were invited to a 'taste-off' between beef and the meat from a twenty-three-year-old horse. A number of dishes were prepared by the same chef, employing equivalent cuts of meat, which were then served side by side. The verdict was unanimous in favour of the horse-meat. One of the tasters, Dr Amédée Latour, declared:

| | |
|---|---|
| *Bouillon de cheval*<br>Surprise générale! C'est parfait,<br>c'est excellent, c'est nourri,<br>c'est corse, c'est aromatique,<br>c'est riche de goût. | *Le bouillon de boeuf* est bon,<br>mais comparativement inférieur,<br>moins accentué de goût,<br>moins parfumé,<br>moins résistant de sapidité. |

The first horse banquet held in Britain was on 19 December 1867, at the St James' Hotel in London. It was prepared by Francatelli, and contained:

*Le Consommé de Cheval aux Quenelles*
*Les Saucisses de Cheval aux Pistaches*
*La Culotte de Cheval braisée aux Choux*

———— A FEW THAI FOOD TERMS ————

| | | | |
|---|---|---|---|
| *Kaeng* | curry | *Plaa* | fish |
| *Tom* | soup | *Phet* | spicy; hot |
| *Khao suay* | steamed rice | *Phat* | stir-fried |
| *Khao phad* | fried rice | *Phrik* | chill |
| *Khao niaw* | sticky rice | *Kung* | prawns/shrimp |
| *Neua* | beef | *Kuaytiaw* | noodles |
| *Muu* | pork | *Manao* | lime |
| *Kai* | chicken | *Yam* | salad |
| *Khai* | egg | *Naam sii-yu* | soy sauce |
| *Ka-ti* | coconut extract | *Khing* | ginger |

—————————— CIGAR AFICIONADOS ——————————

A few of those who have graced the cover of *Cigar Aficionado* magazine:

| | | |
|---|---|---|
| George Burns | Michael Douglas | Dennis Hopper |
| Linda Evangelista | Chuck Norris | Raquel Welch |
| Jack Nicholson | John F. Kennedy | Jeff Bridges |
| Matt Dillon | John Travolta | Rudolph Giuliani |
| Demi Moore | Ernest Hemingway | Kevin Spacey |
| A. Schwarzenegger | Susan Lucci | Don Johnson |
| Wayne Gretzky | Laurence Fishburne | Winston Churchill |
| James Woods | J.P. Morgan | Fidel Castro |
| Claudia Schiffer | Kevin Bacon | The Sopranos |
| Pierce Brosnan | Bo Derek | Tom Selleck |
| Denzel Washington | Gene Hackman | Groucho Marx |
| Sylvester Stallone | Kevin Costner | Danny DeVito |

— TRADITIONAL AMISH FAMILY SEATING PLAN —

|  | MOTHER | *Daughters in ascending order of age* |
|---|---|---|
| FATHER | | |

*Sons in ascending order of age*

—————————— SOYER'S CHRISTMAS FEAST ——————————

The celebrated chef (famously of the London Reform Club) Alexis Soyer helped organise an extraordinary Christmas festival (♭1852) in Ham Yard, Windmill Street, London. To the sound of 'waltzes, polkas, and merry tunes' 22,000 of 'the poorest of the poor' were fed with the following:

| | | | |
|---|---|---|---|
| Roast and baked meat | 9,000lb | Cakes | 50 |
| Beef pies | 178 | Half-quartern loaves | 6,000 |
| Hare pies | 50 | Biscuits | 1 cask |
| Rabbit pies | 60 | Spanish nuts | 1 bushel |
| Pork and mutton pies | 50 | Chestnuts | 18 bushels |
| Roast geese | 20 | Oranges | 6 boxes |
| Whole ox† | 1 | Tea | 6,000oz |
| Potatoes | 3,300lb | Coffee | 9,000oz |
| Porter | 5,000 pints | Sugar | 2,500lb |
| Plum pudding | 5,000lb | † Supplied by the Western Gas Company | |

--------------------- EATING THE ZOO ---------------------

In 1870, during the siege of Paris, the zoo in the Jardin des Plantes was forced to sell the animals it was no longer able to feed. A number of restaurateurs, who had been reduced to serving rat, bought what they could from the cages. The following is the Christmas Day menu (the 99th day of the siege) prepared by Bellanger from the restaurant Voisin's:

*Beurre, radis, sardines* ................ butter, radishes, sardines
*Tête d'âne farcie* ...................... stuffed ass's head
*Purée de haricots rouges aux croutons* ...... purée of red beans with croutons
*Consommé d'éléphant* .................... elephant soup
*Goujons frits* ........................... fried fish
*Le chameau rôti à l'Anglaise* ............ roast camel, English style
*Le civet de kangourou* ................... kangaroo stew
*Côtes d'ours rôties sauce poivrade* ....... roast bear chops in pepper sauce
*Cuissot de loup, sauce chevreuil* ........ haunch of wolf with venison sauce
*Le chat flanqué de rats* ................. cat garnished with rats
*Salade de cresson* ...................... watercress salad
*La terrine d'antelope aux truffes* .......... antelope and truffle terrine
*Cèpes à la Bordelaise* .............. cep mushrooms, Bordeaux style
*Petis pois au beurre* ..................... buttered peas
*Gâteau de riz aux confiture* .............. rice pudding with jam
*Fromage de Gruyère* ..................... Gruyère cheese

WINES: Xérès · Latour Blanche 1861 · Château Palmer 1864
Mouton Rothschild 1846 · Romanée Conti 1858
Bollinger frappé · Grand Porto 1827 · Café et Liqueurs

A personal account of the siege was published by the journalist Albert D. Vandam in *An Englishman in Paris* (*c.*1897). In this text Vandam recalls:

*I have eaten the flesh of elephants, wolves, cassowaries [a kind of ostrich], porcupines, bears, kangaroos, rats, cats, and horses ... The proprietor of the English butcher-shop, M. Debos, who was not an Englishman at all, supplied most of these strange dishes, for he bought nearly all the animals from the Zoological Gardens at tremendous prices ... the elephants were sold to M. Debos for 27,000 Francs.*

--------------- WHISKY, WHISKEY, & USQUEBAUGH ---------------

Whisky derives from the Gaelic term *usquebaugh,* which translates as 'water of life': *uisge* – water; *beatha* – life. In modern usage *whisky* is from Scotland, and *whiskey* is from Ireland (the American spelling is *whiskey*).

## SHAKESPEARE ON FOOD AND LOVE

If music be the food of love, play on;
Give me excess of it, that, surfeiting,
The appetite may sicken, and so die.

— *Twelfth-Night; or, What You Will*, I.i

## THE LOYAL TOAST

By tradition the loyal toast is that raised to the monarch or head of state. (In many gatherings the loyal toast signals that guests may smoke.) In England it is always the first toast proposed at a formal occasion, usually taking the form 'The Queen', though a few areas have modified the toast:

The Channel Islands ..................... *The Queen, Duke of Normandy*
Lancashire .................................. *The Queen, Duke of Lancaster*
Canada ............................. *The Queen*, or *The Queen of Canada*
Isle of Man...................................... *The Queen, Lord of Man*
Australia (since 2000).............. *The Queen and the People of Australia*

A number of military units do not give the loyal toast on the grounds that their devotion to the monarch has been proved in action. For example, the 2nd Battalion KSLI were excused the toast by George IV after officers of the regiment quelled a group of rioters who had insulted him in a Brighton theatre. George IV similarly exempted the Royal Welch Fusiliers (who only raise the loyal toast on St David's Day), since their loyalty could 'never be in doubt' after the 1797 Nore Mutiny. Members of the Royal Navy are permitted to remain seated during the loyal toast when on board ship – either because their loyalty is also beyond question, or because their ships are too cramped to stand safely. Under Cromwell's rule, monarchists expressed their secret allegiance by toasting the 'King of the Jews': a reworking of [I]reland, [E]ngland, [W]ales, and [S]cotland. Jacobites indicated their allegiance to the exiled James II by raising their toast over a glass of water or a fingerbowl – thereby literally and metaphorically toasting the King 'over the water'. It has been claimed that when Queen Elizabeth I visited the Royal Exchange in 1571, Sir Thomas Gresham pledged her health with a cup of wine into which he had mixed the crushed atoms of a pearl reported to be worth in excess of £15,000.

## DUKE HUMPHREY

To 'Dine with Duke Humphrey' is to go without dinner.

—————— SWIFT'S MODEST PROPOSAL ——————

'A Modest Proposal for Preventing the Children of the Poor People in Ireland from Being a Burden to Their Parents or Country, and for Making Them Beneficial to Their Public' was Jonathan Swift's indignant attack on the poverty of the Irish under English government, written in 1729. In what has become a classic satirical text, Swift gives some advice:

> *I have been assured by a very knowing American of my acquaintance in London, that a young healthy child well nursed is at a year old a most delicious, nourishing, and wholesome food, whether stewed, roasted, baked, or boiled; and I make no doubt that it will equally serve in a fricassee or a ragout. [...] A child will make two dishes at an entertainment for friends; and when the family dines alone, the fore or hindquarter will make a reasonable dish, and seasoned with a little pepper or salt will be very good boiled on the fourth day, especially in winter.*

—————— WATER BOILING POINT AT ALTITUDE ——————

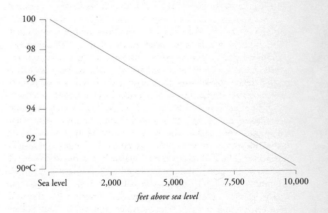

—————— TO MAKE 'RUMFUSTIAN' ——————

*Beat up in a jug, the yolks of two eggs with a tablespoon of sifted sugar; take then half a pint of old Burton ale, one wine-glass of gin, one wine-glass of sherry, a little spice and lemon rind. Let the ale, wine, and gin, mixed together come to the boil, then pour in the egg mixture, whisking rapidly; serve hot with a little nutmeg grated atop.*

───── HAPPY BIRTHDAY, MR PRESIDENT ─────

JOHN F. KENNEDY'S 45TH BIRTHDAY DINNER
19 May 1962

Crabmeat baked in Sea Shell

─────

Chicken Broth with Spring Wheat

─────

Medallions of Beef glazed in Madeira
Herbed Carrots · Woodland Mushrooms

─────

The Presidential Birthday Cake

The dinner was served at the Four Seasons Restaurant in New York; once completed, the guests decamped to a party at Madison Square Gardens, where Marilyn Monroe sang her coquettish version of 'Happy Birthday'.


───────────── CORDON BLEU ─────────────

*Un Cordon Bleu* was a knight of the ancient French order of the *Saint-Esprit* – a nickname deriving from the blue ribbon from which the decoration was suspended. Henry III created the order in 1578, limiting membership to 100 knights; it was the highest order of chivalry under the Bourbon monarchy. The term 'cordon bleu' quickly became associated with excellence in any field and then specifically culinary excellence, although the link between the order and cookery is disputed. Some claim that the blue ribbons of a cook's apron were favourably compared to the blue sash of the knights. Others claim that a few of the knights (such as Comte d'Olonne) became famed as epicures, giving rise to the expression *'Bien, c'est un vrai repas de cordon bleu'*. Nowadays, the phrase usually refers to the Cordon Bleu cookery school founded in Paris in 1895.


───────────── EPICUREAN CALENDAR ─────────────

A curious culinary joke based on the French Revolutionary calendar:

| | | | |
|---|---|---|---|
| January | *Marronglaçaire* | July | *Melonial* |
| February | *Harrengsauridor* | August | *Raisinose* |
| March | *Oeufalacoquidor* | September | *Huîtrose* |
| April | *Petitpoisidor* | October | *Bécassinose* |
| May | *Aspergial* | November | *Pommedetaire* |
| June | *Concombrial* | December | *Boudinaire* |

### Water-Soluble Vitamins

| | | Isolated c. | Rich natural sources | Deficiency can cause | Daily intake (mg) ♂ | ♀ |
|---|---|---|---|---|---|---|
| B1 | thiamine | 1912 | meat, wholegrain cereals | beriberi, depression, polyneuritis | 1·4 | 1·0 |
| B2 | riboflavin | 1933 | milk, eggs, greens, peanuts | bloodshot eyes, skin problems | 1·3 | 1·1 |
| B3 | niacin | 1867 | beef, pork, chicken, wheat | pellagra, diarrhoea, depression | 17·0 | 13·0 |
| B5 | pantothenic acid | 1933 | liver, yeast-based foods | impaired co-ordination, & healing | 6·0 | 6·0 |
| B6 | pyridoxine, etc. | 1934 | potatoes, nuts, liver | depression, ?peripheral neuropathy | 1·4 | 1·2 |
| B12 | cobalamin | 1948 | meat, fish, dairy products | anaemia, irritability | 0·0015 | 0·0015 |
| C | ascorbic acid | 1932 | fruit, vegetables | scurvy, anaemia, bruising | 40·0 | 40·0 |
| Folate | folic acid, etc. | 1941 | green vegetables, chickpeas | anaemia, infections, ?birth defects | 0·2 | 0·2† |

### Fat-Soluble Vitamins

| | | Isolated c. | Rich natural sources | Deficiency can cause | Daily intake (mg) ♂ | ♀ |
|---|---|---|---|---|---|---|
| A | retinol | 1931 | fish, liver, dairy products | night-blindness, low immunity | 0·7 | 0·6 |
| D | ergocalciferol, etc. | 1936 | oily fish, eggs, liver, sunlight | rickets, osteomalacia | varies | varies |
| E | tocopherol, etc. | 1922 | plant oils, nuts, seeds | breakdown of red blood cells | 4·0 | 3·0 |
| K | phylloquinone, etc. | 1934 | green vegetables, cereals | haemorrhage | 0·001 | 0·001 |

### Minerals

| | Isolated c. | Rich natural sources | Deficiency can cause | Daily intake (mg) ♂ | ♀ |
|---|---|---|---|---|---|
| Calcium (Ca) | 1808 | milk, cheese, green veg | weak bones, osteoporosis | 700 | 700 |
| Iron (Fe) | — | liver, meat, green veg, beans | anaemia | 6·7 | 11·4 |
| Magnesium (Mg) | 1828 | leafy vegetables, nuts | depression, cramps | 300 | 270 |
| Phosphorus (P) | 1674 | red meat, dairy, fish, poultry | loss of appetite, weak bones | 550 | 550 |
| Potassium (Na) | 1807 | bananas, vegetables, pulses | diarrhoea, vomiting, weakness | 3,500 | 3,500 |
| Sodium Chloride (NaCl) | — | salt, salty foods, junk food | dehydration, cramps | <6,000 | <6,000 |

(Daily intake levels are approximate for healthy adults · † Higher levels of folic acid may be required during pregnancy · If in doubt, seek medical advice.)

## SPANISH SALADS

According to Spanish proverb, the perfect salad is made by four characters:

| | | | |
|---|---|---|---|
| a SPENDTHRIFT............for oil | a STATESMAN .............for salt |
| a MISER................for vinegar | a MADMAN.................to stir |

## A FEW NOTABLE SAUCES

| SAUCE | CHARACTERISTIC INGREDIENTS |
|---|---|
| Aïoli | *mayonnaise, garlic, lemon juice* |
| Béarnaise | *egg yolks, reduced vinegar, butter, shallots, chervil, thyme, bay* |
| Béchamel | *basic white sauce from flour, boiled milk, butter* |
| Chasseur | *mushrooms, shallots, tomatoes, white wine* |
| Cumberland | *redcurrant jelly, port, orange and lemon zest and juice* |
| Demi-glace | *espagnole reduced with white stock, with wine or Madeira* |
| Espagnole | *brown stock, brown roux, mirepoix, tomato purée* |
| Hollandaise | *emulsion of butter and egg yolks, seasoning, lemon juice* |
| Louis | *mayonnaise, chilli, peppers, spring onions, lemon juice* |
| Marie-Rose | *mayonnaise, tomato ketchup, Worcestershire sauce, Tabasco* |
| Mayonnaise | *emulsion of egg yolk & oil, with vinegar, seasoning, mustard* |
| Pesto | *basil, garlic, pine nuts, Parmesan, olive oil* |
| Reform | *espagnole w. hard egg whites, gherkins, mushrooms, tongue, truffle* |
| Remoulade | *mayonnaise, mustard, gherkins, herbs, capers, (anchovy, egg)* |
| Salsa Verde | *oil, vinegar, garlic, anchovy, capers, parsley* |
| Velouté | *veal, chicken stock or fish fumée thickened with a white roux* |

## RATES OF DIGESTION

The 1898 publication *Ogilvie's Encyclopedia of Useful Information* gives a (far from scientific) chronology of the time taken to digest various foods:

| | | | | | |
|---|---|---|---|---|---|
| Rice...........1 hour | Eggs (boiled).........3 | Cheese ............3½ |
| Milk (raw) ........1¼ | Beef (roast)...........3 | Turnips (boiled) ...3½ |
| Apples.............1½ | Bread (fresh).......3¼ | Fowls (roast).........4 |
| Eggs (raw).........1½ | Carrots (boiled)....3¼ | Cabbage..........4½ |
| Milk (boiled)........2 | Butter .............3½ | Veal (roast) ........5½ |

## AMBIGU

*Ambigu* is an old French term for a meal (such as that served at a ball) at which all the dishes (hot, cold, and dessert) are presented simultaneously.

—————— THE COMIC COOKERY BOOK ——————

Haphazard extracts from *The Comic Cookery Book* by F.H. Curtis, 1891:

### DINNER GIVING

The first thing to be considered is the setting of the table. A round table is best calculated to show off a square meal. [...] It is also considered in poor taste to have the knives and forks chained to the edge of the table. [...] Observe the courtesies of society at table; bright conversation, fun and witticisms are the best aids to digestion. Do not embellish your talk with obituary anecdotes, stories of hangings, and the like.

### CLEAR SOUP

Take two pints of water, wash them thoroughly on both sides, pour into a dish or something and stir round the kitchen until tired. Dilute with ice water, cook until it comes to the boil. Have the boil lanced and serve.

### TO FRY FISH

Remove the works from the interior department, pick off the scales, remove the teeth, and fry in a frying pan – or anything else which fancy dictates.

### TO TELL A BAD EGG

This depends entirely on what you wish to tell the egg. It if be bad news, break gently.

### MUSHROOM SAUCE

Make room for your mush in a saucepan, cut off the stalks and throw them away. Throw the mush after them.

### BEETS

Dead beets should be served in summary manner. Winter beets in a wintry manner. Boil them, and having obtained a supply of hearts, serve two hearts but with a single beet.

### STRAWBERRY ICE-CREAM

Freeze your cream in a slow oven. Line a dish with straw, bury the cream in it. Make it into mounds and serve cold.

### ROAST DUCK

Boil it first until it is legal tender, then unboil it, roast it in the oven.

### POTATOES FOR BREAKFAST

Have it understood that they shall not be eaten the previous evening.

### TABLE MANNERS

Should you be so unfortunate as to upset a glass of claret upon the table cloth, immediately sprinkle the stain liberally with salt to prevent it setting. On the same principle, if you upset the salt, sprinkle it liberally with claret. [...] Do not eat from the end of the spoon with a noisy imitation of a high pressure suction-pump. [...] In carving, should the bird slip from under your knife, do not appear covered with confusion, although you may be with gravy, simple say to the lady in whose lap the bird had landed, 'I'll trouble you for that hen', or words to that effect, and let the autopsy proceed.

## PIECES PER POUND

A rough estimate of the number of pieces of fruit and veg in 1lb (*c.*½kg):

| | | | |
|---|---|---|---|
| Durian | ¼ | Carrots (medium) | 5–7 |
| Grapefruit | 1 | Tomatoes (medium) | 6–7 |
| Peppers (large) | 1 | Plums (medium) | 10 |
| Bananas (medium) | 2–3 | Apricots | 15–18 |
| Pears (medium) | 2–3 | Dates | 20 |
| Apples (medium) | 3–4 | Strawberries | 30–35 |
| Bananas (small) | 3–4 | Button mushrooms | 35 |
| Onions (medium) | 3–4 | Cherries | 35–40 |
| Peaches (medium) | 4–5 | Mangetout | 140 |

## HEIMLICH MANOEUVRE

The Heimlich Manoeuvre, developed in 1976 by Henry J. Heimlich, is an emergency technique to aid someone who is choking, The rescuer hugs the victim from behind, and dislodges the foreign object by employing upward abdominal thrusts. According to the Heimlich Institute, amongst the 50,000 who owe their lives to the manoeuvre are the following 'celebrities': Goldie Hawn, Ronald Reagan, Cher, Elizabeth Taylor, Ed Koch, Dick Vitale, John Chancellor, Carrie Fisher, Jack Lemmon, and Walter Matthau.

## CALORIE EXPENDITURE

Approximate Calories burnt each minute by those weighing *c.*150lb:

| | | | | | |
|---|---|---|---|---|---|
| Sitting still | 1–2 | Yoga | 4–6 | Skipping | 7–9 |
| Snooker | 2–6 | Badminton | 5–6 | Morris dancing | 7–10 |
| Housework | 3–6 | Brisk walking | 5–8 | Tennis | 7–12 |
| Golf | 3–6 | Aerobics class | 5–9 | Football | 7–13 |
| Cricket | 3–7 | Ping-pong | 6–7 | Jogging | 8–13 |
| Fencing | 4–6 | Sex | 6–11 | Langlauf | 8–13 |
| Gymnastics | 4–6 | Swimming | 6–12 | Squash | 8–13 |

These figures are approximate and will vary depending on a number of factors, from how vigorous the gymnastics, to the incline of the hill climbed, or the weight of the golf clubs carried. For every pound over 150lb add 10%; for every pound under 150lb subtract 10%. For an explanation of the Calorie, see p.43. [1 chocolate éclair = *c.*190 Calories]

---------------GARLIC · ALLIUM SATIVUM---------------

❦ Although garlic was banned from the Roman Temple of Cybele, it formed part of the rations of Roman soldiers who chewed it before battles in the hope it might bestow courage. ❦ Pliny claimed garlic prevented madness, repelled snakes, and could counter the magnetic power of the lodestone. ❦ The Batak people of Indonesia consider garlic has the power to recover lost souls. ❦ Carpathian shepherds apparently still protect their flocks against snake-bites by massaging their hands with garlic before they milk their ewes. ❦ In many cultures garlic is said to ward off demons, witches, fairies, and (in India) the 'evil eye'. ❦ Western superstition (heavily influenced by Bram Stoker's *Dracula*, 1897) supposes that garlic wards off vampires. ❦ Many claims have been made for garlic's antiseptic powers and it was often employed by medics during WWI. ❦ Over the years garlic has been said to cure a remarkable range of diseases, including whooping-cough, influenza, ringworm, jaundice, hydrophobia, and even infertility. Recent medical evidence seems to suggest that garlic may play a role in reducing levels of cholesterol. ❦ Horace railed against the stench of garlic, claiming it was 'more harmful than hemlock'. ❦ It has been mooted that the Emperor Nero may have invented the garlic sauce *aïoli*. ❦ In 1300 King Alfonso of Castile forbade knights who had eaten garlic within a month to enter his Court or speak to any courtiers. ❦ Superstitious travellers placed garlic at crossroads to ward off Hecate (Goddess of the Underworld). ❦ Aymara Indian bullfighters in Bolivia take garlic into the ring in the hope it will stop bulls from charging. ❦

### GARLIC IN OTHER LANGUAGES

| | | |
|---|---|---|
| Russian...... *chesnock* | Thai .......... *katiem* | Italian.......... *aglio* |
| Spanish .......... *ajo* | Vietnamese........ *toi* | Malay........ *ku cai* |
| Portuguese....... *alho* | Swedish ....... *vitlök* | Chinese ..... *suen tau* |
| German... *Knoblauch* | Norwegian.... *hvitløk* | French ........... *ail* |

---------------CHIP-SHOP PRICES IN GLASGOW---------------

The following prices are from a Glasgow fish 'n' chip shop (June 2003):

| | | | |
|---|---|---|---|
| Fish | £1·95 | Steak pie | £2·20 |
| Chicken | £2·30 | Mince pie | £1·90 |
| King rib | £2·30 | Deep-fried pizza | £2·00 |
| Smoked sausage | £2·30 | Deep-fried Mars Bar | £2·30 |
| Sausage (x2) | £2·10 | Chips | £0·95 |
| Hamburger | £2·10 | Chips with curry sauce | £1·70 |
| Black pudding | £2·10 | Chips and gravy | £1·40 |
| Haggis | £2·10 | Chips and cheese | £2·20 |

—————— THE JAPANESE TEA CEREMONY ——————

The Japanese tea ceremony, *Cha-no-yu* ('hot water for tea'), is so suffused with delicacy, detail, and complexity as to overwhelm the uninitiated. The ceremony combines Zen philosophy with meditation, spirituality, and deep-rooted senses of tradition, nature, and hospitality. Tea was not cultivated in Japan until seeds were brought into the country from China during the T'ang dynasty (*c.*700), and one of the earliest accounts of a tea ceremony dates back to the Emperor Shomu (724–49). It was not until the Kamakura period (1192–1333) that *Cha-no-yu* developed its elaborate formality. Myo-ei Shonin (*c.*1200), an advocate of the tea ceremony as a central component of a religious life, described the Ten Virtues of Tea:

| | |
|---|---|
| *Has the blessings of all the Deities* | *Strengthens friendship* |
| *Promotes filial piety* | *Disciplines body and mind* |
| *Drives away the Devil* | *Destroys the passions* |
| *Banishes drowsiness* | *Gives a peaceful death* |
| *Wards off Disease* | *Keeps the Five Viscera in harmony* |

The creation of a formal tea etiquette, *temae,* is credited to Murata Shuko (*d.*1503) – the Father of Teaism. Shuko emphasised the spiritual and meditative meaning of *Cha-no-yu* through arrangement, purification, and calmness of mind. *Temae* involves the precise arrangement, cleaning and warming of the tea utensils before the tea is made and served. Depending on the quantity of tea, the heat of the water, and the speed of whisking, the tea can be either thick *(koicha)* or thin *(usucha)*. Different procedures exist for drinking *koicha* and *usucha*. However, both involve formal exchanges; precise methods for handling the bowl and sipping the tea; and polite appreciation both of the tea and the utensils which were used.

*Skill in* Cha-no-yu *consists in making guests enjoy themselves. Expertise in serving tea consists in doing it so that there is nothing to notice.*
Matsudaira Fumai (*fl.*1800)

*In Tea the host is simplicity and the guest elegance.*
Matsudaira Naritada (*c.*1830)

*Tea is not only the antidote to drowsiness,*
*but one of the ways whereby man may return to his source.*
Lu Yu (733–804)

The complexity of *Cha-no-yu* is hard to exaggerate. Every detail, from the location and architecture of the tea-house to the movements of the tea-master, coalesces to influence the character of each unique ceremony – summed up by the phrase *ichi go ichi e* – one chance in one's lifetime.

## ——— DOUBLE, DOUBLE, TOIL AND TROUBLE ———

Ingredients used by the three witches in Shakespeare's *Macbeth* IV.i:

Poison'd entrails · toad · fillet of a fenny snake · eye of newt
toe of frog · wool of bat · tongue of dog · adder's fork
blind-worm's sting · lizard's leg · howlet's wing · scale of dragon
tooth of wolf · witches' mummy · maw and gulf of ravin'd salt-sea shark
root of hemlock digg'd i' the dark · liver of blaspheming Jew
gall of goat · slips of yew · nose of Turk · Tartar's lips
finger of birth-strangled babe · tiger's chaudron · baboon's blood

## ——— DIETING QUOTATIONS ———

BARBARA CARTLAND · The right diet directs sexual energy into the parts that matter.

DIANA, PRINCESS OF WALES · Eating disorders, whether it be anorexia or bulimia, show how individuals can turn the nourishment of the body into a painful attack on themselves and they have at the core a far deeper problem than mere vanity.

ANDY ROONEY · The biggest seller is cookbooks and the second is diet books – how not to eat what you've just learned how to cook.

JEAN KERR · I feel about airplanes the way I feel about diets. It seems to me that they are wonderful things for other people to go on.

MASON COOLEY · Dieting is our last tie with asceticism.

MARY EVANS YOUNG · You have a situation where girls of eight want to lose weight and at twelve they can tell you the fat content of an avocado … but they don't know what constitutes a healthy meal.

ROSEMARY CONLEY · As the low-fat diet unfolded, I really felt that God was showing me the way.

ROBERT MORLEY · *(on why he was opposed to diets)* If people take the trouble to cook, you should take the trouble to eat.

ROCHEFOUCAULD · To safeguard one's health at the cost of too strict a diet is a tiresome illness indeed.

## ——— BALLS ———

As is the case with offal (see p.70), when testicles appear on menus they tend to nestle behind coy euphemisms: *stones* or *fries* in England; *criadillas* in Spain; *prairie oysters* in America; *testicoli* or *granelli* in Italy; *Hoden* in Germany; and *rognons blancs, animelles,* or *frivolités* in France.

—— SOME ITALIAN PASTA SHAPES ——

FUSILLI · spirals of pasta originally formed by wrapping spaghetti around knitting needles

PENNE · hollow pasta quills cut diagonally into short tubes

GNOCCHI · shaped and marked to resemble potato gnocchi

FUSILLI COL BUCO · Thin spirals the length of spaghetti

PAPARDELLE · wide ribbons of pasta

FARFALLE · bow-tie or butterfly shapes of thin pasta ideal for sauces or layered dishes

RADIATORI · small 'radiators' of ridged pasta

FETTUCCINI · flat ribbon noodles, similar to TAGLIATELLE

RAVIOLI · small parcels of pasta stuffed with various fillings

RIGATONI · ridged, short tubes of pasta, akin to MACARONI

CASARECCIA · small twisted s-bends

TORTELLINI · stuffed pasta shapes moulded into rings

CAPPELLETTI · small circles of pinched hat-shaped pasta

## ——— SOME ITALIAN PASTA SHAPES ———

CANNELLONI · pipes of pasta which are stuffed and then baked or covered with sauce

GENOVESINI · diagonally cut short tubes, similar to PENNE

BUCATINI · thick, hollow spaghetti

CAMPANELLE · frilly pasta bells, ideal for sauces

NIDI · nests of TAGLIATELLE which unravel when cooked

RUOTI · small wheel-shapes of pasta

MACARONI · hollow tubes of pasta

AGNELLOTTI · parcels of stuffed pasta in various shapes

CONCHIGLIE · shells of pasta in a variety of sizes

MAFALDE · flat noodles with jagged edges

LUMACHE · snail-shaped pasta shells

AMORI · hollow, ridged pasta spirals

There is, of course, a vast array of other Italian pasta shapes, from tiny pasta stars *(stellini)* to wide flat sheets *(lasagne)*. Furthermore, pasta is enjoyed across the world in a wide variety of forms: Spanish *fideos*, a form of thin vermicelli; Austrian *Kasnudln*, stuffed square pasta; Jewish *lokshen*, egg noodles akin to tagliatelle; Siberian *pel'meni*, semi-circular pasta filled with meats; Chinese *wontons*, deep-fried pasta parcels; and so on.

When thou hast eaten and art full, then thou shall bless
the Lord thy God for the good land which he hath given thee.
DEUTERONOMY 8:10

Lord, forgive us that we feast while others starve.
BISHOP CHARLES GORE (1853–1932)

Et hic Episcopus cibum et potum benedicit.
*And here the Bishop blesses the food and drink.*
BISHOP ODO · THE BAYEUX TAPESTRY, SECTION 51

Let us with a gladsome mind,
Praise the Lord, for He is kind.
All things living He doth feed,
His full hand supplies their need,
For His mercies aye endure
Ever faithful, ever sure.
JOHN MILTON (1608–74)

Here a little child I stand,
Heaving up my either hand;
Cold as Paddocks† though they be,
Yet I lift them up to Thee,
For a Benizon to fall
On our meat and on us all.
ROBERT HERRICK (1591–1674)

Be thankful for the least gift, So shalt thou be
meet [ready] to receive the greater.
THOMAS À KEMPIS (1380–1471)

Dominum Jesus sit potus et esus. · *Lord Jesus be drink and food.*
MARTIN LUTHER (1483–1546) [attrib.]

May God give us thankful hearts and keep us in friendship
and brotherly love to our lives' end.
THE MERCHANT TAYLORS' COMPANY

Heavenly father, keep us alive, There's ten for dinner and food for five.
ANONYMOUS C19th

God Save the King, Bless our dinners, Make us thankful.
ADMIRAL LORD NELSON (1758–1805) [attrib.]

God is great, God is good, Let us thank Him for our Food.
JIMMY CARTER'S WHITE HOUSE GRACE

God send this crumb well down.
A jocular Royalist grace at the expense of Oliver Cromwell

†Paddocks are toads. See also Jewish blessings on p.107; and 'The Selkirk Grace', p.17.

## GOUT

Gout is a metabolic disorder characterised by painful attacks of joint inflammation – the first sign of the disease is often extreme pain in the innermost joint of the big toe. Gout tends to affect men over the age of forty, and is caused by deposits of monosodium urate monohydrate crystals in the joints. The term 'gout' derives from the French for 'drop' *(goutte)* and the ancient belief that the pain associated with the disease was caused by acidic humours *(noxa)* percolating into the joints. It tends to be assumed that gout is a disease of the aristocracy brought on by overindulgence. In *The Devil's Dictionary* (1906), Ambrose Bierce defined gout as 'a physician's name for the rheumatism of a rich patient'. Havelock Ellis wrote in *A Study of British Genius* (1904) that gout was an indication of 'pre-eminent intellectual ability'. Yet while alcohol, rich foods, and a sedentary life-style may exacerbate the condition, it seems that gout is largely caused by inherited biochemical abnormalities. Indeed teetotallers and vegetarians also suffer from the disease – as Thomas Sydenham noted (*c.*1728): 'if you drink wine you have the gout and if you do not drink wine the gout will have you'. Recent research suggests that the consumption of cherries might help guard against attacks of gout.

A wine merchant sent a bottle of sherry to Lord Chesterfield, claiming that it had powers to cure gout. His Lordship replied with a note stating:

> *Sir, I have tried your sherry and frankly prefer the gout.*

## SOME EDIBLE FLOWERS

marjoram · thyme · hyssop · bergamot · sage · mint · hollyhock
chive · dill · lavender · daisy · rose · borage · camomile · citrus
saffron · courgette · rocket · fennel · fuchsia · sunflower · dandelion
primrose · hibiscus · tiger lily · basil · evening primrose · rosemary
clover · nasturtium · viola · thyme · marigold

Eliza Smith's orange-flower brandy recipe from
*The Compleat Housewife* (*c.*1729):

> *Take a gallon of French Brandy, boil a pound of orange flowers
> a little while, and put them in, save the water and with
> that make a syrup to sweeten it.*

[It should be noted that certain individuals may suffer adverse reactions to flowers and that, as with all food, care should be taken with known sensitivities and allergic reactions. Some flowers are highly poisonous: rhododendron, wisteria, laburnum, and *many* others should not be eaten. If in doubt, seek specialist advice before cooking or consuming.]

---

## CUBAN CIGAR SIZES

A wide nomenclature of Cuban cigar sizes exists, of which these are a few:

| Size | length (inches) | ring gauge | example gauge sizes |
|------|-----------------|------------|---------------------|
| Demi-Tasse | 3⅞ | 30–2 | |
| Trés Petit Corona | 4–4⅝ | 34–42 | *panetela* |
| Panetela | 4½–4⅞ | 26 | |
| Petit Corona | 5 | 42 | |
| Robusto | 5 | 50 | |
| Corona | 5½ | 42 | *corona* |
| Piramide | 5½–6⅛ | 52 | |
| Belicoso | 5½–6⅛ | 52 | |
| Corona Gorda | 5⅝ | 44–46 | |
| Corona Extra | 5⅝ | 44–46 | |
| Laguito No.2 | 6 | 38 | *double corona* |
| Lonsdale | 6¾ | 42 | |
| Coronas Grandes | 5–6¾ | 42–43 | |
| Churchill | 7 | 47 | |
| Laguito No.1 | 7½ | 38 | |
| Double Corona | 7⅝ | 49 | |
| Gran Corona | 9¼ | 47 | |

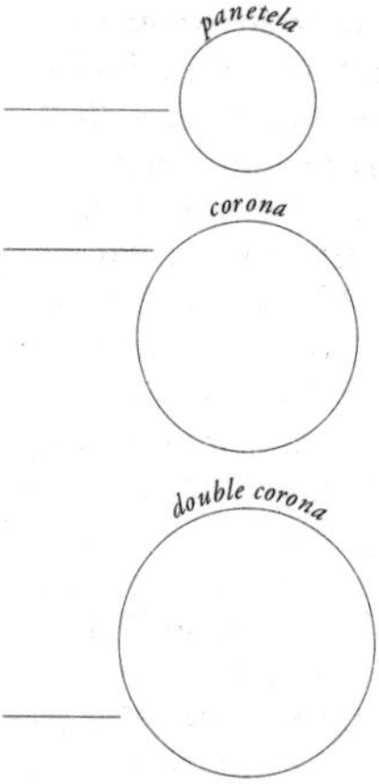

*Ring gauges are expressed in 64ths of an inch · Variations in size exist between manufacturers.*

---

## WINE TEMPERATURES

An indication of the temperatures (ºC) at which wines might be served:

| | | | |
|------|------|------|------|
| Light sweet white wine | 5–8 | Light red wine | 11–12 |
| Sparkling wine | 6–9 | Full dry white | 13–16 |
| Fino sherry | 8–10 | Madeira, port | 13–15 |
| Light dry white | 9–12 | Full-bodied red | 15–18 |
| Rosé | 8–10 | Fine Burgundy | 15–17 |
| Sherry | 10–11 | Fine Bordeaux | 16–18 |

---

## GANDHI'S DIET

In 1929, Gandhi described his daily diet in a letter to *Young India*:

8 tolas of germinating wheat · 8 tolas of green leaves pounded
8 tolas of sweet almonds reduced to a paste
6 sour lemons · 2 ounces of honey

*The* tola *was based on the weight of the old rupee coin – approximately 0·4oz or 11g.*

--- VATEL & SUICIDE ---

François Vatel was a French chef celebrated for his elaborate banquets and credited with the invention of many dishes – including *Crème Chantilly.* Vatel was lured from the employ of Nicolas Fouquet by Louis, Prince of Condé, for whom he acted as a culinary master of ceremonies. The zenith of Vatel's career should have been in 1671 when Condé invited Louis XIV to a stay at Chantilly Castle (with the intention of touching the King for money). However, on the first night, much to Vatel's horror, there was insufficient meat to feed an unexpected influx of guests, and fireworks worth 16,000F failed to explode. For the events of the next day, we can turn to a contemporaneous letter written by Madame Marie de Sévigné:

> *[Vatel] rose at four the next morning, determined to attend to every-thing in person. He found everybody asleep. He meets one of the infe-rior purveyors, who brought only two packages of sea-fish: he asks, 'Is that all?' 'Yes, Sir.' The man was not aware that Vatel had sent to all the seaports. Vatel waits some time … his brain begins to burn; he believed that there would be no more fish. He finds Gourville; he says to him, 'Monsieur, I shall never survive this disgrace.' Gourville made light of it. Vatel goes up stairs to his room, places his sword against the door, and stabs himself to the heart; but it was not until the third blow … that he fell dead. The fish, however, arrives from all quarters; they seek Vatel to distribute it; they go to his room, they knock, they force open the door; he is found bathed in his own blood.*

Vatel is not the only chef to have taken his own life after a perceived culinary failure. In 1966 Alain Zick shot himself in the head on learning that his Paris restaurant *Relais des Porquerolles* had lost a Michelin star. In 2003, a similar escape was sought by Bernard Loiseau when the score of his Michelin three-star Burgundian restaurant *Côte d'Or* was downgraded from 19/20 to 17/20 in the *GaultMillau* guide. Loiseau, who had been awarded the French Legion of Honour in 1995, once claimed 'we are selling dreams. We are merchants of happiness'. However, according to a fellow chef, he had also threatened 'if I lose a [Michelin] star, I will kill myself'.

--- DOMINO'S PIZZA TOPPINGS ---

Domino's Pizza has outlets in more than sixty countries and, in order to cater for local tastes, they offer toppings specific to a number of locations:

| Topping | Country | Topping | Country |
| --- | --- | --- | --- |
| *Squid* | Japan | *Capsicum* | Australia |
| *Tuna & Sweet Corn* | England | *Crème Fraîche* | France |
| *Black Bean Sauce* | Guatemala | *Lamb & Pickled Ginger* | India |
| *Barbecued Chicken* | The Bahamas | *Linguica & Chorizo* | Portugal |
| | | *Grilled Lamb* | Netherlands |

## THE ETYMOLOGY OF CLARET

In current oenological usage 'claret' is an English synonym for the red wines of Bordeaux. Claret's etymology is uncertain but it seems to derive from light-red or yellowish wines like the French *vin clairet*. As far back as 1398 the word was employed to describe hippocras – wine mixed with honey and sweet spices. Later, claret was merely descriptive of anything (especially wine) with a dark red hue – which explains why claret has been a slang term for blood since *c*.1604. Samuel Johnson (with all the certainty of a reformed drinker) stated that 'a man may choose between abstemiousness and knowledge, or claret and ignorance'. However, Dr Johnson was not always right – as we learn from the film *Diamonds Are Forever*. Here, James Bond discovers that his waiter is a hired goon when he is ignorant of the provenance of Château Mouton Rothschild 1955:

*... for such a grand meal I had rather expected a claret.*
James Bond

*Of course. Unfortunately, our cellars are rather poorly stocked with clarets.*
Mr Wint

*Mouton Rothschild is a claret...*
James Bond

## TRADITIONAL FOOD SEASONS

The notion of foods being 'in season' seems antiquated in today's global food market. The following chart gives English seasons from the 1950s:

| | |
|---|---|
| Apples ............ *September–May* | Plums ........... *August–September* |
| Apricots ......... *August–September* | Quinces ........ *October–November* |
| Asparagus ........... *February–July* | Raspberries ........ *June–September* |
| Cardoons .............. *April–May* | Red cabbage ... *September–January* |
| Carrots ................. *May–June* | Sorrel .................... *April–July* |
| Cauliflowers .... *March–November* | Spinach ......... *March–December* |
| Celery ....... *September–February* | Strawberries ....... *June–September* |
| Cucumbers ....... *May–September* | Tomatoes ....... *March–December* |
| French beans ........ *July–October* | Walnuts ...... *September–December* |
| Gooseberries (ripe) ...... *June–July* | |
| Kale ............. *December–March* | *Live in each season as it passes;* |
| Mulberries ...... *August–September* | *breathe the air, drink the drink,* |
| Oranges ........... *November–June* | *taste the fruit, and resign yourself to* |
| Parsnips .......... *September–April* | *the influences of each.* |
| Pears ............ *August–December* | – Henry David Thoreau (1817–62) |

## ——FOOD & DRINK OF THE BAY CITY ROLLERS——

The Bay City Rollers classic 1974 album *Rollin'* features a host of timeless
hits including *Shang-a-Lang,* and *Summerlove Sensation.* The sleeve-notes
from this album describe the band members' favourite foods and drinks:

| | | |
|---|---|---|
| *Well-done steak* | Alan Longmuir | *dark rum & peppermint* |
| *Curries* | Derek Longmuir | *Coke; milk* |
| *Plaice au gratin; roast duck* | Les McKeown | *Cointreau with lemon & lime* |
| *Steak pie and chips; hamburgers* | Stuart Wood | *Coke* |
| *Salad; yoghurt; peach flambé.* | Eric Faulkner | *vodka; wine; tea* |

The sleeve-notes also tabulate the likes and dislikes of the Bay City Rollers: Alan dislikes
'forward people'; Derek dislikes 'poseurs and rain'; Les dislikes 'jealousy and drain-pipe
trousers'; Stuart dislikes 'cold weather and pizza pies' but likes 'meeting people and
staying in hotels'. Eric likes 'lively audiences & Alan's singing' but dislikes 'Brewer's yeast'.

## —————— HIERARCHY OF GASTRONOMY ——————

GASTRONOME
GOURMET
FRIAND (*epicure*)
GOURMAND
GOULU (*glutton*)
GOINFRE (*greedy-guts*)

| GOURMAND | GOURMET |
|---|---|
| one whose chief pleasure is eating | a connoisseur of food and wines |

## —————— COFFEE AND ECONOMICS ——————

Two of Britain's oldest financial institutions were founded in London
coffee-shops. The insurance market Lloyd's of London originated in
Edward Lloyd's coffee-house in Tower Street (later Lombard Street). And
the London Stock Exchange can claim to owe its existence to a coffee-
shop established by Jonathan Miles (*c.*1680) in Exchange Alley, Cornhill.
As early as 1694 Jonathan's accepted subscriptions to John Briscoe's Land
Bank, and the writer John Houghton reported that 'the Monied Man
goes among the brokers (which are chiefly upon the Exchange), and at
Jonathan's Coffee House ... and asks how stocks go?'. In 1698, when
dealers in stocks and shares were eased out of the sedate Royal Exchange
they quickly found a home at Jonathan's. By 1709 The *Tatler* had written
that Jonathan's Coffee House was 'the general market of stock jobbers'.

## VITAMINS IN BEER

According to *The Wiley Encyclopedia of Food Science and Technology* a 'typical' [unspecified] American beer contains the following vitamins:

| Vitamin | %RDA in 1l | mg/l | | | |
|---------|-----------|------|---|---|---|
| | | | Pantothenic Acid ... 25 ........ 1·0 | | |
| | | | Pyridoxine .......... 20 ........ 0·5 | | |
| Thiamine .......... <2 ...... 0·02 | | | Biotin .............. 7 ...... 0·007 | | |
| Riboflavin .......... 20 ........ 0·3 | | | Cyanocobalamin .... 3 ........ 0·1 | | |

## PRISON FOOD

The Prison Service is responsible for feeding Britain's 67,000 prisoners three meals a day, served at the following times *(with some local variations)*:

*breakfast* 07:30–09:00 · *midday* 12:00–14:00 · *evening* 17:00–19:30

Fourteen hours is the longest a prisoner may go without being served food. Prisons must offer inmates high-quality food which is nutritious and safe; certain foods must be offered at these minimum frequencies:

*Daily* – meat; vegetables; fresh fruit · *Twice weekly* – poultry; fish

In addition, prisons must be able to cater for a wide range of religious, medical, and cultural diets including: vegetarian, vegan, Buddhist, Mormon, Ethiopian Orthodox, Hindu, Jewish, Jain, Muslim, and Sikh. The following are a few sample menus provided by the Prison Service:

| SUNDAY | TUESDAY |
|--------|---------|
| *Jerked Chicken* | *Chicken Tandoori* |
| *Lamb with Turmeric Rice* | *Grilled Gammon & Pineapple* |
| *Creamy Vegetable Pie* | *Vegetable Lasagna* |
| *Bean Goulash* | *Vegetarian Sausage Roll* |
| | |
| MONDAY | WEDNESDAY |
| *Special Chicken Fried Rice* | *Lamb Chilli Pie* |
| *Cottage Pie* | *Chicken Tandoori* |
| *Ocean Surprise* | *Leek & Pepper Flan* |
| *Vegetable Chilli* | *Plain Omelette* |

## RIDDLE OF CLARET

A riddle of claret comprises thirteen bottles: one magnum, twelve quarts.

——————— ROASTING TIMES ———————

| Meat | | Time (oven 190°C · 375°F · GAS 5) | Internal temp. |
|---|---|---|---|
| LAMB | rare | 20 mins per 450g + 20 mins | 60–70°C |
| | medium | 25 mins per 450g + 25 mins | 70–75°C |
| | well done | 30 mins per 450g + 30 mins | 75–80°C |
| BEEF | rare | 20 mins per 450g + 20 mins | 60°C |
| | medium | 25 mins per 450g + 25 mins | 70°C |
| | well done | 30 mins per 450g + 30 mins | 80°C |
| PORK | | 35 mins per 450g + 35 mins | 80–85°C |
| CHICKEN | | 20 mins per 450g + 20 mins | 80–85°C |
| TURKEY | | 25 mins per 450g + 20 mins | |
| PHEASANT | | 25 mins per 450g | |
| VENISON | | 25 mins per 450g | |
| HARE | | 20 mins per 450g | |
| WILD BOAR | | 20 mins per 450g | |
| QUAIL | | 20 mins | |
| ORTOLAN | | 15 mins | [450g = 1lb] |

ADVICE: Ensure that any meat which has been frozen is completely defrosted before cooking. Cook stuffing separately (i.e. outside the bird) to ensure that it is fully cooked. Leave roasts to rest in a warm place for 10–20 minutes after removing them from the oven. Ensure that all food is fully cooked and piping-hot before serving. Use an instant-read thermometer placed into the centre or thickest part of the meat to check that the minimum internal temperature has been reached. For poultry ensure the juices run clear, i.e. when the meat is pierced with a knife no blood runs out. If in any doubt *do not serve food undercooked*, and refer to the meat's packaging instructions, or your oven's manual.

——————— HERBS AND SPICES IN LATIN ———————

### HERBS

Basil ........... *Ocimum basilicum*
Bay leaves ........... *Lauris nobilis*
Chervil ....... *Anthriscus cerifolium*
Chives ...... *Allium schoenoprasum*
Coriander.... *Coriandrum sativum*
Dill ........ *Puecedanum graveolens*
Marjoram .... *Origanum majorana*
(Apple) Mint . *Mentha rotundifolia*
Oregano ........ *Origanum vulgare*
Parsley ....... *Petroselinum crispum*
Rosemary .. *Rosemarinus officinalis*
Sage ............... *Salvia officinalis*
Tarragon .. *Artesemisia dranunculus*
Thyme ........... *Thymus vulgaris*

### SPICES

Allspice ............ *Pimenta dioica*
Caraway............... *Carum carvi*
Cardamom *Elettaria cardamomum*
Cinnamon ......... *Cinnamomum zeylanicum*
Clove......... *Eugenia caryophyllus*
Coriander..... *Coriandum sativum*
Cumin....... *Cuminum cyminum*
Ginger .......... *Zingiber officinale*
Nutmeg ......... *Myristica fragrans*
Saffron .............. *Crocus sativus*
Sesame.......... *Sesamum indicum*
Turmeric ...... *Curcuma domestica*
Vanilla ............ *Vanilla fragrans*

—————— THE NOBEL BANQUET ——————

Since 1901 the Nobel Prize ceremony and banquet have taken place on 10 December, the anniversary of Alfred Nobel's death. The banquet is attended by the Laureates, the Swedish royal family and government, and around 1,300 guests. The menu, currently devised by the Chef of the Year Association of Sweden, is kept a secret until the last minute. Below are the menus from the first Nobel banquet, and its counterpart a century later:

|  —— 1901 —— | —— 2001 —— |
|---|---|
| *Hors d'œuvre* | *Homard sur purée de chou-fleur et gelée de langoustines, salade de salicornes* |
| *Suprême de barbue à la normande* | *Caille farcie au foie gras et sa poêle des cèpes et tomates sechées, asperges vertes et purée de cerfeuil* |
| *Filet de bœuf à l'impériale* | |
| *Gelinottes rôties, salade d'Estrée* | *Duo des glace vanille et parfait cassis meringue* |
| *Succès Grand Hôtel, pâtisserie* | WINES |
| | *1989 Louise Pommery Champagne* |
| WINES | *1997 Château Palmer Margaux* |
| *Niersteiner 1897* | *1998 Bernkasteler Badstube* |
| *Château Abbé Gorsse 1881* | *Riesling Eiswein Mosel-Saar-Ruwer* |
| *Champagne Crème de Bouzy* | *Café · Grönstedts Rarissime* |
| *Doux et Extra Dry* | *Grand Champagne* |
| *Xerez* | *Cointreau* |
| | *Eau minérale de Ramlösa* |
| The Peace Prize was jointly awarded to Jean Henri Dunant and Frédéric Passy. | The Peace Prize was jointly awarded to the United Nations and Kofi Annan. |

In recent years two foods do not appear at Nobel banquets. Pork is not served for reasons of cultural sensitivity. Venison is not served because King Carl XVI Gustaf hosts a private dinner for Laureates on 11 December at which he serves a deer that he himself has killed.

—————— CHAMPAGNE CASCADE ——————

The optimum ratio in which to stack glasses for a champagne cascade is:

Base – 60    1st tier – 30    2nd tier – 10    3rd tier – 4    4th tier – 1

## —— KIDDUSH: BLESSINGS FOR WINE & BREAD ——

### — THE JEWISH BLESSING FOR WINE —

בָּרוּךְ אַתָּה, יְיָ אֱלֹהֵינוּ מֶלֶךְ הָעוֹלָם בּוֹרֵא פְּרִי הַגָּפֶן

'Bar-uch Atar Adonai, Elo-henu melech ha-olam, borey p-ree ha-gafen'

We praise You, O Lord our God, King of the universe, Creator of the fruit of the vine

### — THE JEWISH BLESSING FOR BREAD —

בָּרוּךְ אַתָּה יְיָ אֱלֹהֵינוּ מֶלֶךְ הָעוֹלָם הַמּוֹצִיא לֶחֶם מִן הָאָרֶץ

'Bar-uch Ata Adonai, Elo-henu melech ha-olam, hamotzi lech-em min ha-arets'

We praise You, O Lord our God, King of the universe, bringer of bread from the Earth

---

## —— BLUE FOOD ——

It is often said that there are no blue foods in nature [see also *Smarties* p.82] – however, according to P.L. Simmonds in *The Curiosities of Food* (1859):

> *the bluish flesh of the toucan, notwithstanding its enormous and unsightly beak, is a wholesome and delicate meat; and there are no birds that give the Trinidad epicure a more delicious meal.*

---

## —— DRINKING IN THE PALACE OF WESTMINSTER ——

Bars within the Palace of Westminster operate without licence and with no reference to the hours or other regulations imposed by the Licensing Acts. This curious legal exemption has been tested on a number of occasions, and was settled in the 1934 case *R v Graham-Campbell, ex parte Herbert*. Here the King's Bench adjudicated that it could not interfere with the internal operations of the House. As a consequence, the bars within the Palace are able to serve alcohol at any time and, by convention, stay open as long as the Commons is sitting. There are a number of bars in the Palace of Westminster, each of which has a specific membership:

The Pugin Room.........................*Members and Officers, and guests*
Members' Smoking Room................................*Members only*
Strangers' Bar...................*Members, Officers, senior staff, and guests*
Terrace Bar..........................*as for Strangers' Bar* (open Easter–July)
Annie's Bar........................*Members, Officers, and Lobby journalists*
Press Bar..............*Lobby journalists, official report staff, and doormen*

## SPLICING THE MAINBRACE

'Splice the Mainbrace' is the order given within the Royal Navy to issue an extra tot of rum[†] or grog to the men. (Grog is rum diluted with water, named after the C18th admiral 'Old Grog' Vernon.) It seems the phrase derives from the hazardous job of repairing the rigging's main brace. The order can be given by commanding officers and the monarch (the Queen Mother also issued the order on occasion). In recent times the order has been issued when Queen Elizabeth II reviewed the fleet during the Silver Jubilee of 1977; in 1981 to commemorate the marriage of the Prince and Princess of Wales; and in 2002 to celebrate the Queen's Golden Jubilee.

† The Navy's rum ration was abolished in July 1970 by the 1st Sea Lord Admiral 'Ginger' Le Fanu. (In response to his order, the Admiral's nickname swiftly became 'Dry Ginger'.)

## MR BURNS'S LUNCH

Montgomery 'Monty' Burns, wizened plutocratic owner of Springfield's nuclear plant, gives Homer Simpson his antiquarian luncheon order:

*...a single pillow of Shredded Wheat, some steamed toast, and a dodo egg.*

## FOOD AND PREGNANCY

Experts recommend pregnant women EXCLUDE soft mould-ripened cheese (Brie, Camembert, etc.), pâtés, uncooked or under-cooked ready-prepared meals, raw eggs, or food with raw or partially cooked eggs. CAUTION should be exercised with food in general to ensure that it is properly cooked; this is especially the case with sausages and minced meat. While some advocate the exclusion of ALCOHOL, others allow no more than one or two units a couple of times a week. Most experts recommend limiting CAFFEINE intake to around 300mg per day. All experts recommend that pregnant women should avoid both SMOKING and recreational DRUGS completely.

## ORDERING STEAK

| ENGLISH | FRENCH | ITALIAN | SPANISH | GERMAN |
|---------|--------|---------|---------|--------|
| *very rare* | *bleu* | *molto al sangue* | *muy poco hecho* | *'englisch'* |
| *rare* | *saignant* | *al sangue* | *poco hecho* | *blutig* |
| *medium* | *à point* | *al puntino* | *mediano hecho* | *halb durch* |
| *well done* | *bien cuit* | *ben cotto* | *muy hecho* | *durchgebraten* |

## ——— BREAD IN IDIOM ———

Those *on the breadline* live a *bread and cheese* existence unable to *break bread* with others or even to fill their hungry *breadbaskets*. Unless, that is, a *breadwinner* knows *which side his bread is buttered on* and decides to *use his loaf* and *cast his bread upon the water*. Such a *bread and butter* way of life can be brightened by the *bread and circuses* of popular entertainment – without doubt *the greatest things since sliced bread* – yet entertainment always seems to cost a lot of *bread*, and one cannot help but feel that some people are only able to *earn a crust* by *taking the bread out of one's mouth*.

## ——— COGNAC NOMENCLATURE ———

The grading and naming of cognacs is a complex matter since, although minimum legal requirements exist, houses have considerable flexibility in how they name their product. A very basic nomenclature is as follows:

| Term | Years old | Term | Years old |
| --- | --- | --- | --- |
| *** or VS | 2–5 | XO or Napoleon | 6–20 |
| VSOP | 4½–10 | Extra or Grand Reserve | 20–40 |
| | | (2 years is the minimum legal aging time) | |

Over the centuries, a wide range of terms has been employed to describe brandy in general and cognac in particular. Terms like VSOP, XO, XSO and VFOP are all based on the following nomenclature of initials:

| | | | | | | | |
| --- | --- | --- | --- | --- | --- | --- | --- |
| E | extra | M | mellow | P | pale | V | very |
| F | fine | O | old | S | superior | X | extra |

## ——— GHEE ———

Ghee is the traditional cooking fat of Indian cuisine. It is obtained by heating butter – while constantly stirring – until most of the water has evaporated and a richly flavoured fluid is left. The ghee is left to stand before being strained through muslin to remove any sediment. Ghee from buffalo is cream-coloured, whilst ghee from cows is golden yellow – 'like amber' according to the poet Annaji. Ghee is said to be strengthening, and improving of the mind and intellect, and it was considered by Buddha to be one of the foods 'full of soul qualities'. It is of particular use in cooking, thanks to its rich, unsalted flavour and its high smoke point.

Ghee that is kept for between 10 and 100 years is called *kumbhaghrta*.
Ghee that is kept for over 100 years is called *mahaghrta*.
*[Both are considered to have healing properties.]*

## HERMAN MELVILLE ON EATING WHALES

The fact is ... the whale would by all hands be considered a
noble dish, were there not so much of him; but when you
come to sit down before a meat-pie nearly one hundred feet
long, it takes away your appetite.  — *MOBY-DICK*, 1851

## RECIPE FOR A WINTER SALAD

Two large potatoes, passed through a kitchen sieve,
Unwonted softness to a salad give.
Of mordant mustard add a single spoon;
Distrust the condiment which bites so soon;
But deem it not, thou man of herbs, a fault
To add a double quantity of salt.
Three times the spoon with oil of Lucca crown,
And once with vinegar procured from town.
True flavour needs it, and the poet begs,
The pounded yellow of two well-boiled eggs.
Let onion atoms lurk within the bowl,
And, scarce suspected, animate the whole;
And lastly, on the flavoured compound toss
A magic teaspoon of anchovy sauce.
Then, tho' green turtle fail, tho' venison's tough,
And ham and turkey are not boiled enough,
Serenely full the Epicure may say –
Fate cannot harm me –  I have dined today.

— REVD SYDNEY SMITH (1771–1845)

## SOME WORLD BEERS OF NOTE

| | | | |
|---|---|---|---|
| *Presidente*.... | Dominican Republic | *Obolon Premium*.......... | Ukraine |
| *Castle Lager* .......... | South Africa | *Prestige Stout*................. | Haiti |
| *Tinima* ....................... | Cuba | *Quilmes*.................. | Argentina |
| *Cisk Lager*.................... | Malta | *Rüütli Olu*................. | Estonia |
| *Efes Pilsen*................... | Turkey | *Sagres*.................... | Portugal |
| *Hite*.................. | South Korea | *Sapporo*..................... | Japan |
| *Hue Beer* ................. | Vietnam | *Star Beer* .................... | Nepal |
| *Keo* ......................... | Cyprus | *Tiger Beer*.............. | Singapore |
| *Krakus Zywiec*.............. | Poland | *Tsingtao*...................... | China |
| *Cobra*....................... | India | *Victoria Bitter*............ | Australia |
| *Maccabee* .................... | Israel | *Xingu*........................ | Brazil |

# ABSINTHE

Know by a host of aliases – *the green fairy, bottled madness, the green curse, the queen of poisons* – absinthe is a potent green liqueur (60–80% alcohol) flavoured with a variety of aromatic herbs such as angelica, dittany, sweet-flag root, and star anise. However, it is wormwood *(Artemisia absinthium)* which provides absinthe with the notorious hallucinogenic properties which have caused it to be banned in a host of countries, and which have made the drink popular with generations of artists, poets, and writers:

ERNEST HEMINGWAY · ... that opaque, bitter, tongue-numbing, brain-warming, stomach-warming, idea-changing, liquid alchemy.

MAURICE BARRYMORE · Absinthe is the paregoric [medicine] of second childhood.

ERNEST DOWSON · Absinthe makes the tart grow fonder.

OSCAR WILDE · Absinthe has a wonderful colour, green. A glass of absinthe is as poetical as anything in the world. What difference is there between a glass of absinthe and a sunset?

MARIE CORELLI · There ... you have the most marvellous cordial in all the world – drink and you will find your sorrows transmuted – yourself transformed.

GEORGE SAINTSBURY · Absinthe burns like a torchlight procession ... I never myself drank more than one absinthe in a day.

PAUL VERLAINE · ...it was upon absinthe that I threw myself, absinthe day and night.

VOLTAIRE · The first month of marriage is the honeymoon. The second is the absinthe moon.

However, not all of those who have tried absinthe have been so effusive:

JORIS-KARL HUYSMANS · Even when made less offensive by a trickle of sugar, absinthe still reeks of copper, leaving on the palate a taste like a metal button slowly sucked.

DR VALENTIN MAGNAN · In absinthism the hallucinating delirium is most active, most terrifying, sometimes provoking reactions of an extremely violent and dangerous nature.

According to Alec (brother of Evelyn) Waugh, absinthe has a potentiating effect, doubling the potency of everything drunk afterwards. And the neurotoxic power of absinthe has long been known. The Bible mentions these powers several times, warning '...and the third part of the waters became wormwood; and many men died of the waters...' [Revelation 8:10]

*(Ominously, in some Slavic languages wormwood translates as chernobyl.)*

--------- CURRY ---------

The history of curry is much disputed, though most commentators conclude that the curries so enjoyed in Britain bear only a casual relationship with 'authentic' Indian food. The term curry derives initially from the Tamil for spiced sauce *(kari)* – via Canarese *(karil)*, Portuguese *(caril)*, and French *(cari)*. Its earliest usage in English dates to the 1590s. Below are some of the popular curries found in Anglo-Indian restaurants:

| Type | Characteristic Ingredients | Heat [1-5] |
|------|----------------------------|------------|
| BALTI | *slow-cooked in a heavy metal wok* | varies |
| BHUNA | *dry with a rich coconut sauce* | 2 |
| BIRIANI | *spicy, rice-based curry* | varies |
| CEYLON | *with coconut, lemon, and chilli* | 3 |
| DHANSAK | *almost sweet dish served with a lentil purée* | 3 |
| DOPIAZA | *made with lots of onions* | 3 |
| JALFREZI | *green peppers, chillis, and onions* | 3 |
| KARAHI | *dry, sizzling, with onion, and tomatoes* | 3 |
| KASHMIR | *sweet curry with fruit, often lychee* | 3 |
| KORMA | *creamy curry, often with almonds* | 1 |
| MADRAS | *with tomatoes, almonds, lemon juice and chilli* | 4 |
| PASANDA | *creamy with coconut and almonds* | 1 |
| PHAL | *chillis, and more chillis: stupidly hot* | 6 |
| RHOGAN JOSH | *usually lamb, with yogurt, chilli, and tomatoes* | 4 |
| THAL | *a varied selection of dishes* | varies |
| TIKKA MASALA | *ever-popular aromatic, creamy curry* | 1 |
| VINDALOO | *sour with tomatoes, chilli, and potatoes* | 5 |

------ GOWERS-ROUND'S RULES FOR WAITERS ------

Polymath and bon-viveur Sir Wilfred Gowers-Round (1855–1945) became so infuriated by the poor quality and general insolence of waiters that he proposed what he termed a 'manifesto of rules' for waiting staff to follow:

[1] ............... A waiter's job is to serve, and *never* to interpose himself
[2] .................... The ultimate goal of waiting is *inconspicuous service*
[3] ..... Waiters *must* be clean and smart, and should *never* wear Cologne
[4] ............ Under *no circumstances* should a waiter ever *touch* a diner
[5] ............................... Wine-glasses should *never* be filled too full
[6] ........................... Unasked-for advice should *never* be proffered
[7] ............ If diners are content to pour the wine themselves, *let them*
[8] ..... Unless asked, no plates should be removed until *all* have finished
[9] ............... Women diners should be afforded respect *equal* to men
[10] ............... The bill should be placed on the table *without ceremony*

## POLITICAL FOOD QUOTATIONS

CHARLES DE GAULLE · How can anyone govern a nation that has two hundred and forty-six different kinds of cheese?

MARIE ANTOINETTE · *On being told the people had no bread:* Let them eat cake! [attrib.]

TALLEYRAND · England has 3 sauces and 360 religions; this is in contrast to France which has 3 religions and 360 sauces.

JOHN F. KENNEDY · The war against hunger is truly mankind's war of liberation.

JOHN MAJOR · Let me say this. Fine words butter no parsnips!

NAPOLEON BONAPARTE · [attrib.] An army marches on its stomach.

TALLEYRAND · One plans better around a white cloth than around a council table.

JUVENAL · *Duas tantum res anxius optat, panem et circenses.* (Two things only do the people desire anxiously: bread and circuses.)

HERMANN GOERING · We have no butter ... but I ask you – would you rather have butter or guns? ... preparedness makes us powerful. Butter merely makes us fat.

WINSTON CHURCHILL · There is no finer investment ... than putting milk into babies.

EDMUND BURKE · Having looked to government for bread, on the very first scarcity they will turn and bite the hand that fed them.

## CAIPIRINHA AND CACHAÇA

Cachaça is a sugar-cane spirit (around 38–54% alcohol by volume) that forms the key ingredient of the Caipirinha – the national cocktail of Brazil. Caipirinhas are made by mashing half a lime with a teaspoonful of sugar in the bottom of a tumbler before adding a shot of cachaça and filling the glass with crushed ice. Cachaça has many nicknames in Brazil, one of which – Parati – derives from the name of the elegant colonial town famous not only for producing the spirit, but also for hosting South America's leading literary festival: *Festa Literária Internacional de Parati.*

## SOME OIL SMOKE POINTS

| Oil | °C | °F | Oil | °C | °F |
|---|---|---|---|---|---|
| Sunflower oil | 200 | 392 | Olive oil | 210 | 410 |
| Corn oil | 210 | 410 | Soya oil | 210 | 410 |
| Groundnut oil | 210 | 410 | Rapeseed oil | 225 | 437 |
| | | | Grapeseed oil | 230 | 446 |

———— SOME FOOD & DRINK PROVERBS ————

One man's meat is another man's poison
Remember, a little of what you fancy does you good
A sharp stomach makes short devotion
If you can't stand the heat, get out of the kitchen
So long as there's water, there's tea
After dinner, sit a while; after supper, walk a mile
*Chi ben sena ben dorme* · Who sups well sleeps well
Never forget — Quick to the feast, quick to the grave
*Toute chair n'est pas venaison* · Not all flesh is venison
Too many cooks spoil the broth
Bacchus drowns more than Neptune
*Pain tant qu'il dure, vin à mesure* · Eat at pleasure, drink by measure
God sends meat and the devil sends cooks
Hunger makes the best sauce
He who drinks beer thinks beer, and he who drinks wine thinks wine[†]
You can't eat your cake and have it [sic]
*Qui medice vivat, misere vivat* · To live for the doctor is no life at all
Better to pay the butcher than the doctor
Use first Dr Quiet, then Dr Merriman, and Dr Diet[§]
Diet cures more than the lancet
*Der Mensch ist, was er isst* · Man is what he eats
A good stomach is the best sauce
Sauce for the goose is sauce for the gander
Wilful waste makes woeful want
*A tavola non bisogna aver vergogna* · Never be ashamed to eat your meat
You dig your grave with your teeth
*Kila nyama nyama tu* · Every meat is meat
Out of the frying pan, into the fire
*Tu pulmentaria quaera sudando* · Seek relishes by sweating toil[‡]
Don't cry over spilt milk
An apple a day keeps the doctor away
By suppers more have been killed than Galen ever cured
*Fabas indulcat fames* · Hunger sweetens beans
Enough is as good as a feast, and better than a surfeit
You can't get butter out of a dog's mouth
Mickle corn, mickle care
He that will steal an egg will steal an ox
Good tea cannot be too hot, nor good beer too cold
Unless the kettle boiling be, filling the teapot spoils the tea
*Verba non alunt familiam* · Words won't support a family
He that masters his thirst, masters his health

———

[†] Longfellow, *Hyperion* [Bk.iv · Ch.3]; [§] ?Jonathan Swift; [‡] Horace, *Satires* [Bk.II].

## VARRO ON DINNER PARTIES

The Roman scholar and writer, Marcus Terentius Varro (116–27BC) declared that the number of guests at a dinner party should not be fewer than the number of Graces [3], nor greater than the number of Muses [9].

## TIPPING GUIDE

Although which services are considered worthy of tipping varies around the world, most countries tip restaurant waiting staff 10–20% of the bill.

| Sum | 12½% | 15% | 20% | Sum | 12½% | 15% | 20% |
|---|---|---|---|---|---|---|---|
| 5 | 0·63 | 0·75 | 1·00 | 105 | 13·13 | 15·75 | 21·00 |
| 10 | 1·25 | 1·50 | 2·00 | 110 | 13·75 | 16·50 | 22·00 |
| 15 | 1·88 | 2·25 | 3·00 | 115 | 14·38 | 17·25 | 23·00 |
| 20 | 2·50 | 3·00 | 4·00 | 120 | 15·00 | 18·00 | 24·00 |
| 25 | 3·13 | 3·75 | 5·00 | 125 | 15·63 | 18·75 | 25·00 |
| 30 | 3·75 | 4·50 | 6·00 | 130 | 16·25 | 19·50 | 26·00 |
| 35 | 4·38 | 5·25 | 7·00 | 135 | 16·88 | 20·25 | 27·00 |
| 40 | 5·00 | 6·00 | 8·00 | 140 | 17·50 | 21·00 | 28·00 |
| 45 | 5·63 | 6·75 | 9·00 | 145 | 18·13 | 21·75 | 29·00 |
| 50 | 6·25 | 7·50 | 10·00 | 150 | 18·75 | 22·50 | 30·00 |
| 55 | 6·88 | 8·25 | 11·00 | 155 | 19·38 | 23·25 | 31·00 |
| 60 | 7·50 | 9·00 | 12·00 | 160 | 20·00 | 24·00 | 32·00 |
| 65 | 8·13 | 9·75 | 13·00 | 165 | 20·63 | 24·75 | 33·00 |
| 70 | 8·75 | 10·50 | 14·00 | 170 | 21·25 | 25·50 | 34·00 |
| 75 | 9·38 | 11·25 | 15·00 | 175 | 21·88 | 26·25 | 35·00 |
| 80 | 10·00 | 12·00 | 16·00 | 180 | 22·50 | 27·00 | 36·00 |
| 85 | 10·63 | 12·75 | 17·00 | 185 | 23·13 | 27·75 | 37·00 |
| 90 | 11·25 | 13·50 | 18·00 | 190 | 23·75 | 28·50 | 38·00 |
| 95 | 11·88 | 14·25 | 19·00 | 195 | 24·38 | 29·25 | 39·00 |
| 100 | 12·50 | 15·00 | 20·00 | 200 | 25·00 | 30·00 | 40·00 |

## SUGAR IN WINE

Many sparkling wines are naturally very dry and in order to balance the flavour additional sugar is added. Below are some of the sugar limits:

| Sparkling wine description | Additional sugar g/l | | |
|---|---|---|---|
| Extra brut | <6 | Extra dry | 12–20 |
| Brut | <15 | Sec | 17–35 |
| | | Demi-sec | 33–50 |
| | | Rich / doux | >50 |

———— BEZOARS ————

Bezoars are collections of abnormal matter which form within the stomach or small intestines. Commonly found in animals (especially grass-eating ruminants) bezoars have been traditionally prized for their 'magical' powers. For example, *Lapis bezoar orientale*, obtained from the stomachs of antelopes and Persian wild goats was considered to be particularly effective against poison. (The word bezoar derives from Persian *badzahr: bad* meaning 'against', and *zahr* meaning 'poison'.) In rare cases, usually associated with psychiatric disorders, bezoars occur in human beings. If bezoars grow to form an obstruction they may require surgical removal. Three classical types of human bezoar are recognised:

*Trichobezoar* ........................................... a collection of hair
*Phytobezoar* ...................... a collection of fruit and vegetable matter
*Trichophytobezoar* ..... a collection of hair and fruit and vegetable matter

—— SCHEMATIC OF LEONARDO'S LAST SUPPER ——

Bartholomew · James the Less · Andrew · Judas · Peter · John · Jesus · Thomas · James the Great · Philip · Matthew · Thaddeus · Simon

*see Salt, p.133

———— BIRD'S NEST SOUP ————

A Chinese delicacy for centuries, bird's nest soup (as the name suggests) is made from the nesting materials of a number of South Asiatic swifts – commonly *Collocalia whiteheadi*. Since these nests are usually made in inaccessible rocks and caves their acquisition is extremely hazardous and their price commensurate. Nests are usually harvested in March and most respectable collectors wait until any eggs have hatched – though from time to time 'nest wars' break out between harvesters and poachers. The nests are constructed from twigs, seaweed, saliva, and mucus – and the various methods of cooking involve soaking and cleaning the nests before slowly simmering to extract the flavour. One elaborate recipe involves stuffing a nest inside a chicken that is then boiled to create clear broth.

—————————— FRIDGE & FREEZER STORAGE ——————————

– MAXIMUM RECOMMENDED FRIDGE STORAGE TIMES –

| Product | Days (approx) |
| --- | --- |
| Milk | 4–5 |
| Cheese, soft | 2–3 |
| Cheese, hard | 7–14 |
| Fruit juice, freshly squeezed | 1–2 |
| Eggs, raw[§] | 14 |
| Vegetables, cooked | 2 |
| Potatoes, cooked | 2 |
| Joints (e.g. lamb, beef), cooked | 3 |
| Joints (e.g. lamb, beef), raw | 3 |
| Ham, cooked | 2 |
| Casserole, cooked | 2 |
| Sliced meat, cooked | 2 |
| Fish, cooked | 1 |
| Fish, raw | 1–2 |
| Poultry, raw | 2 |
| Sliced meat, raw | 2 |
| Mince, raw | 1 |
| Sausages, raw | 3 |
| Bacon, raw | 7 |

(§ Ideally, eggs should be stored in a fridge.)

*Fridge safety advice:* Be careful not to overload the fridge, as this can cause the temperature to rise above safe levels · Store raw and uncooked food in covered containers to avoid the possibility of their contaminating cooked food · Allow hot food to cool naturally before putting it in the fridge · Check regularly that the temperature of the fridge is below 5ºC (41ºF).

– MAXIMUM RECOMMENDED FREEZER STORAGE TIMES –

| Product | Months (approx) |
| --- | --- |
| Cream | 6–7 |
| Cheese, hard | 4–5 |
| Cheese, soft | 3–4 |
| Ice-cream | 3–5 |
| Beef | 4–6 |
| Chicken | 10–12 |
| Lamb | 4–5 |
| Pork | 4–6 |
| Venison | 10–11 |
| Minced beef | 3–4 |
| Green vegetables | 10–12 |
| Tomatoes | 6–7 |
| Fruit juice | 4–5 |
| Bread | 2–3 |
| Ready-prepared meals[†] | 2–5 |
| Oily fish | 3–4 |
| White fish | 6–7 |

(Times are for an average domestic freezer.)

† Highly seasoned & spicy ready-prepared meals may need to be kept for shorter periods.

*Freezer safety advice:* If in *any* doubt as to the storage time of a product, check the packaging or the freezer manual · Ensure that food is labelled identifying both date and contents · Store raw food separately underneath cooked food · Ensure that the freezer temperature is below -18ºC (-4ºF).

Shop-bought frozen food has instructions on how long it may be kept in a freezer. The following is a guide based on the freezer compartment stars:

*[-6ºC] ......... 1 week   **[-12ºC] ..... 1 month   ***[-18ºC] .. 3 months

## ——— IMPERIAL TO METRIC CONVERSIONS ———

| — WEIGHT— | | — LENGTH — | | — VOLUME — | |
|---|---|---|---|---|---|
| *ounces* | *grams* | *inches* | *cm* | *imperial* | *ml* |
| ¼ | 7 | ⅛ | 0·3 | ¼ tsp. | 1·25 |
| ½ | 14 | ¼ | 0·6 | ½ tsp | 2·5 |
| ¾ | 21 | ½ | 1·2 | 1 level tsp | 5 |
| 1 | 28 | ¾ | 1·9 | ½ tbsp. | 7·5 |
| 2 | 57 | 1 | 2·5 | 1 level tbsp. | 15 |
| 3 | 85 | 1¼ | 3 | 1 fl.oz | 30 |
| 4 *or* ¼lb | 114 | 1½ | 4 | 2 fl.oz | 60 |
| 5 | 142 | 2 | 5 | 4 fl.oz | 120 |
| 6 | 170 | 2½ | 6 | ¼ pint | 142 |
| 7 | 199 | 4 | 10 | ⅓ pint | 189 |
| 8 *or* ½lb | 227 | 5 | 12·5 | ½ pint | 284 |
| 9 | 255 | 6 *or* ½ft | 15 | ¾ pint | 426 |
| 9½ | 270 | 7 | 18 | 1 pint | 568 |
| 10 | 284 | 8 | 20·5 | 1¼ pints | 710 |
| 10½ | 298 | 9 | 23 | 1½ pints | 852 |
| 12 *or* ¾lb | 341 | 10 | 25·5 | 1¾ pints | 1 litre |
| 14 | 397 | 12 *or* 1ft | 30·5 | 2 pints | 1·3 litres |
| 16 *or* 1lb | 454 | 2ft | 61 | 3 pints | 1·7 litres |
| 2¼lb | 1kg | 3ft | 91·5 | 3½ pints | 2 litres |
| 4½lb | 2kg | 4ft | 122 | 1 gallon | 4·5 litres |
| (14lb = 1*stone* = 6·4kg) | | 5ft | 152·5 | 2 gallons | 9 litres |

Conversions have been rounded. Never mix metric and imperial measures in one recipe.

## ——— AMERICAN CUP CONVERSIONS ———

| *One cup* | *grams* | | |
|---|---|---|---|
| | | Mince | 240 |
| | | Onions, chopped | 115 |
| Butter [1 stick] | 110 | Peas | 150 |
| Butter; lard; margarine | 225 | Potatoes, mashed | 230 |
| Button mushrooms | 120 | Potatoes, sliced | 170 |
| Cabbage, sliced | 80 | Rice, cooked | 150 |
| Chopped nuts | 120 | Rice, uncooked | 200 |
| Cornflour | 125 | Semolina; couscous | 180 |
| Currants | 150 | Sugar, brown | 180 |
| Flour | 150 | Sugar, caster | 230 |
| Golden syrup | 350 | Sugar, icing | 130 |
| Grated cheese | 110 | Sultanas; raisins | 200 |
| Jam | 230 | Tomatoes | 230 |

## ALCOHOL MEASURES

| BEER | | SPIRITS | |
|---|---|---|---|
| nip | ¼ pint | tot [whisky] | ⅙, ⅕, ¼, or ⅓ gill |
| small | ½ pint | noggin | 1 gill |
| large | 1 pint | bottle | 1⅓ pints |
| flagon | 1 quart | | **GILL** |
| anker | 10 gallons | 1 gill | ¼ pint |
| tun | 216 gallons | modern pub measures | (see p.122) |

## TEMPERATURE CONVERSIONS

To convert ° Celsius to ° Fahrenheit........ multiply by 1·8 and add 32
To convert ° Fahrenheit to ° Celsius...... subtract 32 and divide by 1·8
Approximate reversible temperatures....... 16°C ≈ 61°F · 28°C ≈ 82°F
Water boils at................ 100°C; 212°F; 80°Réaumur; 373·1 Kelvin
Water freezes at.................... 0°C; 32°F; 0°Réaumur; 273·1 Kelvin

## OVEN TEMPERATURES

| Description | °C | °F | Gas Mark | Aga† |
|---|---|---|---|---|
| very slow | 110 | 225 | ¼ | very cool |
| | 120 | 250 | ½ | |
| | 140 | 275 | 1 | |
| slow | 150 | 300 | 2 | cool |
| | 160–70 | 325 | 3 | warm |
| moderate | 180 | 350 | 4 | |
| | 190 | 375 | 5 | medium |
| moderate hot | 200 | 400 | ·6 | medium high |
| | 220 | 425 | 7 | |
| hot | 230 | 450 | 8 | high |
| very hot | 240–60 | 475 | 9 | very high |

† 'Aga' is an acronym derived from the maker: *Svenska [A]ktienbolaget [G]as[a]kumulator Co.*

## APOTHECARIES' CONVERSIONS

| WEIGHTS | | MEASURES | |
|---|---|---|---|
| 20 grains | 1 scruple | 20 minims | 1 fl. scruple |
| 3 scruples | 1 drachm | 3 fl. scruples | 1 fl. drachm |
| 8 drachms | 1 ounce | 8 fl. drachms | 1 fl. ounce |
| 12 ounces | 1 pound | 20 fl. ounces | 1 pint |

## SUGAR STAGES

| Name | °F | °C | Culinary uses |
|---|---|---|---|
| COATED | 212 | 100 | *coating fruits in sugar* |
| SMALL THREAD | 217–21 | 103–05 | *almond paste* |
| THREAD | 223–36 | 106–13 | *icings, butter cream* |
| SOFT BALL | 234–40 | 112–16 | *fondant, marzipan* |
| FIRM BALL | 224–50 | 118–21 | *toffee, caramel* |
| HARD BALL | 250–66 | 121–30 | *Edinburgh rock* |
| SOFT CRACK | 270–90 | 132–43 | *butterscotch, rock* |
| HARD CRACK | 300–10 | 149–54 | *acid drops, candy floss* |
| LIGHT CARAMEL† | 320–38 | 160–70 | *praline, brittle* |
| DARK CARAMEL | 350–60 | 176–82 | *colouring, sauces* |

† The Arabs have been credited with inventing caramel – the Arabic *Qandi* means 'crystallised sugar'. One of caramel's early applications was as a depilatory in harems.

## NAPKIN-FOLDING: 'THE VICTORY'

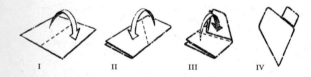

I      II      III      IV

## EATING DOGS

There are a number of methods for preparing dog – although the risk of trichinosis makes it imperative for hounds to be cooked thoroughly. Hawaiians and Samoans traditionally cooked dogs in ground ovens (the hair having been removed by singeing with hot stones). The Chins of Burma apparently stuffed their dogs with rice before boiling them whole. Mayans traditionally raised small, hairless, mute dogs *(techichis)* specifically for consumption, castrating them at birth to make them fatter. The Chinese cure legs of dog *(la tsan)* with rock-salt and sesame seeds, or stir-fry them with ginger and bean-curd *(Nan taso go zo)*. Indonesian recipes exist for dog marinaded in coconut-cream *(saté bumbu dendeng)*; and the Swiss at one time had a taste for carpaccio of dried dogmeat *(Gedörrtes Hundefleisch)*. The Vietnamese simmer dog-steaks with wine; and in the Philippines dogmeat stew *(Adobo aso)* is made with garlic, vinegar and chicken. According to the writer Porphyry (AD234–305) the Greeks developed their taste for dog by accident during an animal sacrifice. Having performed the service a priest chanced to lick his fingers; he so enjoyed the flavour that he then feasted on the burnt remains.

## HANGOVER CURES

*'The wrath of grapes'* — JEFFREY BERNARD on hangovers

Since alcohol was first imbibed – and its residual effects suffered – a noble, distinguished (almost alchemical) search for the ultimate hangover cure has been underway. The homoeopathic principle of *similia similibus curantur* ('like cures like') lies behind 'hair of the dog that bit you' remedies which seem to have included everything from straight brandy to a spicy Bloody Mary. Some of the more elaborate hangover remedies are:

THE DOCTOR · Raw egg, brandy, sugar, fresh milk. (Sherry may be substituted.)

THE EMBALMER · A pint of cold tea mixed with slices of lemon.

THE COALMAN · Melt butter over hot water, stir in a dessertspoonful of Worcester sauce, the same quantity of orange juice, a pinch of cayenne, and about half a wineglassful of old port. Take some freshly browned toast and soak in the mixture before eating.

CHAMPAGNE · Regularly cited as the ultimate hangover cure. Some recommend adding a splash of brandy, others a couple of raw eggs – when the concoction become a SURGEON-MAJOR.

THE SCORCHER · Brandy, lemon juice, cayenne pepper.

ST MARK'S PICK ME UP · 10 drops of Angostura bitters, 10 drops of orange bitters, a glass of brandy, two glasses water, a shot of curaçao, lemon juice. Mix well.

THE NURSE-MAID · A schooner of sherry poured into half a pint of cold milk, seasoned with cloves.

THE BATHING CURE · A series of baths – ice cold and as hot as can be borne – in alternation.

BRAZIL RELISH · ½ curaçao, one raw egg, fill with maraschino.

THE LAZENBY · Hot water infused with ginger, cloves and honey.

*(The Ancient Greeks believed that* AMETHYST *was an antidote to intoxication and they prized highly drinking-vessels made from the stone.)*

## SOME JAPANESE VEGETABLE CUTS

| | | | |
|---|---|---|---|
| *mijin giri* | finely shredded | *hyoshi giri* | cut into batons |
| *sainomo giri* | cut into dice | *sen giri* | very fine julienne cut |
| *senmen giri* | cucumber fan cut | *tanzaku giri* | thin rectangular cut |
| *sogi giri* | long, thin diagonal cut | *hangetsu giri* | half round cut |
| *hana giri* | petalled flower cut | *icho giri* | quarter round cut |

## —— UNITS AND CALORIES IN ALCOHOL ——

| Drink | Measure | Typical Units | Typical Calories |
|---|---|---|---|
| Cider, medium | 1 pint | 2 | 200 |
| Cider, strong | 1 pint | 3–4 | 260–400 |
| Lager/beer, medium | 1 pint | 2 | 180 |
| Lager/beer, strong | 1 pint | 3–4 | 280–440 |
| Alcopops | 275ml | 1½–2 | 100–250 |
| Port & sherry | 25ml (⅙ gill) | 1 | 40 |
| Spirits | 25ml (⅙ gill) | 1 | 50 |
| Wine, 9% | 125ml | 1 | 90 |
| Wine, 12% | 125ml | 1½ | 90 |
| Wine, 14% | 125ml | 2 | 100 |

Many pubs serve spirits (etc.) in 35ml or 50ml measures. Wine is often served in glasses exceeding 125ml. 'Home' measures tend to be more generous. A 750ml bottle of wine holds six 125ml glasses. A unit of alcohol is defined as 8g by weight, or 10ml by volume, of pure alcohol. The British government's advice is that men should drink no more than 3–4 units, and women no more than 2–3 units, on any particular day.

## —— SHELF LIFE OF SOME CANNED GOODS ——

| Goods | Months |
|---|---|
| Sauerkraut | 14 |
| Grapefruit pieces | 18 |
| Okra | 18 |
| Berries | 18 |
| Mushrooms | 20 |
| Peas | 20 |
| Apple Juice | 24 |
| Apricots | 24 |
| Fruit cocktail | 24 |
| Plums | 24 |
| Asparagus | 24 |
| Spinach | 24 |
| Tomatoes | 24 |
| Figs | 24 |
| Peaches | 27 |
| Pears | 28 |
| Apples | 30 |
| Carrots | 30 |

*(Months are approximate.)*

## ——ROSEMARY & CHRISTMAS——

Rosemary *(Rosmarinus officinalis)* was a popular Christmas decoration in the 19th century. St Thomas More said of it: ''Tis the herb sacred to remembrance and therefore to friendship'; the choirboys of Ripon carried it on Christmas morning as a sign of redemption. A number of legends link rosemary with Christmas: it is said that the herb's purple hue derives from the robes of the Virgin Mary; that its aroma comes from the swaddling clothes of Christ; that the plant will never grow taller than Christ; and that if a rosemary bush lives longer than Christ's 33 years, it will branch outwards not upwards. Because of these associations with Mary, it is said that rosemary grows best 'where the mistress is master'.

## SOME SALADS OF NOTE

CAESAR SALAD · cos lettuce and croutons, usually served with Parmesan, anchovies, olive oil, lemon juice, raw egg, Worcester-shire sauce

PANZANELLA · bread salad with tomatoes, peppers, cucumbers, onions, basil, capers, anchovies and olives

RUSSIAN SALAD · a mixture of cooked diced potatoes with peas, carrots, green beans and mayo served on lettuce and garnished with hard-boiled eggs, gherkins and beetroot

SALADE NICOISE · a salad that is variously selected from: tuna, tomatoes, cucumbers, broad beans, (cooked French beans), hard-boiled eggs, anchovy fillets or tuna, black olives, basil, parsley: often dressed with a garlic vinaigrette

WALDORF SALAD · a mixed salad with apples, (lemon juice), celery, walnuts, all bound together with a thin mayonnaise [probably the creation of Oscar Michel Tschirky, the *maître d'* of New York's Waldorf Astoria Hotel for a special supper in 1896]

BRUNSWICK SALAD · sliced sausage with tomato, grated apple, cooked French beans, and pickled gherkins, dressed with parsley and vinaigrette

COBB SALAD · turkey or chicken often with lettuce, bacon, hard-boiled eggs, avocado, tomatoes, cheese and a vinaigrette dressing

GREEN GODDESS · lettuce with endive, spring onions, cloves and anchovies, with tarragon vinegar, and mayonnaise – topped with chicken, crab-meat or shrimps

## KITCHEN CABINET

The term 'kitchen cabinet' – meaning an unofficial inner group of political advisers – has been associated with a number of administrations from Lloyd George's in the 1920s to Harold Wilson's in the 1970s. A number of explanations for the term have been proposed, perhaps the most likely of which dates to the 1830s and the American President Andrew Jackson, who held private meetings of political confidants in the White House kitchens. However, it is possible that the term (or its concept) actually originates in the C17th, and the Commonwealth. Oliver Cromwell's wife Elizabeth suffered endless mockery from Royalists for her domestic outlook. She was accused of running the Court like a merchant's wife, and directing her husband's politics from the kitchen. After the Restoration these attacks intensified in a series of plays and publications. In 1664 Thomas Milbourn even went so far as to publish a satirical cookery book entitled *The Court and Kitchin of Elizabeth*, in which he accused Cromwell's wife of corruption, bribery, and theft, and declared that she was 'an hundred times fitter for a Barn than a Palace'.

--------------------- STREET CRIES ---------------------

Joseph Addison wrote in the *Spectator* (251; 1711) 'there is nothing which
more astonishes a Foreigner, and frights a Country Squire, than the Cries
of London'. A few of these cries, common to many major cities, included:

> *Buy my Dish of great Eels!* · *Hott baked Wadens* [stewed pears] *Hott!*
> *Fair Lemons and Oranges!* · *Buy my fat Chikens!*
> *H-a-ansome cod! Best in the market! All alive! all alive! Alive-O!*
> *Any Kitchen Stuffe have you, Maids!* · *Twelve Pence a Peck, Oysters!*
> *Delicate Cowcumbers to Pickle!* · *Worcestershyr Salt!*
> *Quick periwinckels!* · *Buy my live goose!* · *Hot pesecodes!* [pea pods]
> *Dumplings Ho!* · *Whose for a Mutton pie, or an Eel pie?*
> *Buy a new Mis-seleny!* · *Six-pence a pound, Fair Cherryes!*
> *New born Eggs, eight-a-groat!* · *Hot Spice Gingerbread!*
> *Wall Fleet Oysters!* · *Rue, Sage, and Mint – farthing a bunch!*
> *Barcelona Philberts!* [hazel-nuts] · *Lilly White Mussels – penny a quart!*
> *Lilly White Vinegar!* · *Ripe Speregas!* [asparagus]
> *Any Tripe, or Neat's-foot, or Calf's-foot, or trotters ho!*
> *Had-had-had-had-haddick! All fresh and good!*

The strain of continuous repetition often caused the cries to become
indistinct. J.T. Smith claimed the cry of '*Holloway Cheese Cakes*' sounded
for all the world like '*All my teeth ache*'. Addison accused the street
vendors of being deliberately obscure so as to mislead the public. A.W.
Tuer was more understanding: 'If vegetables are sometimes a little stale,
or fruit is suspiciously over-ripe, they do not perhaps feel absolutely called
upon to mention these facts; but they give bouncing penn'orths, and their
clients are generally shrewd enough to take good care of themselves.'

--------------- TROLLOPE ON WINE AND REALITY ---------------

> *Who can always drink Lafitte of the finest, can always talk*
> *to a woman who is both beautiful and witty, or can always find*
> *the right spirit in the poetry he reads? A man has usually to work through*
> *much mud before he gets his nugget.*

— Can You Forgive Her?, Ch.XVII

> *It may be said that nothing in the world is charming unless it be achieved*
> *at some trouble. If it rained '64 Leoville – which I regard as the most divine*
> *of nectars – I feel sure that I should never raise it to my lips.*

— Ayala's Angel, Ch. XVII

## ——— 1920s DÉBUTANTE DANCE CARD ———

The after-dinner dances performed at the débutante coming-out party of 'Leonora' [surname unknown] on 6 January 1926, from the archives of the celebrated royal printers Frank Smythson Ltd, of Bond Street, London:

| | | | |
|---|---|---|---|
| Fox Trot | *Alabamy Bound* | Fox Trot | *Hong Kong* |
| Fox Trot | *Susie* | Fox Trot | *Yearning* |
| Fox Trot | *My Sugar* | Fox Trot | *Waiting for the moon* |
| Fox Trot | *Ukelele lady* | Valse | *I love the moon* |
| Valse | *Rose Marie* | One Step | *Sweet little you* |
| Fox Trot | *Yes, Sir, that's my baby* | Fox Trot | *Dipping in the moonlight* |
| Fox Trot | *Paddelin' Maddelin* | Fox Trot | *Oriental Moon* |
| One Step | *Toy Drum Major* | Valse | *The lost world* |
| Fox Trot | *Tell me more* | Fox Trot | *You're so near & yet so far* |
| Valse | *When you and I were 17* | Medley | [Music by *The Gardinians*] |

## ——— SOME NOTABLE VEGETARIANS ———

A few who have practised (to a greater or lesser extent) a vegetarian diet:

| | | |
|---|---|---|
| Percy Bysshe Shelley | Loretta Swit | Brigid Brophy |
| Adolf Hitler† | St Clare | Benjamin Franklin |
| Paul McCartney | John Harvey Kellog | Upton Sinclair |
| Leonardo da Vinci (?) | Luigi Cornaro | James Coburn |
| Gandhi | John Wesley | Susan St James |
| Pythagoras | G. Bernard Shaw§ | Leo Tolstoy |
| Sir Stafford Cripps | John Howard | Ed Begley, Jr. |
| Richard Wagner | Linda Blair | Alicia Silverstone |
| St Francis of Assisi | John Frank Newton | Woody Harrelson |
| St David | Annie Besant | Tippi Hedren |
| Malcolm Muggeridge | Albert Schweitzer | George Harrison |

† Hitler's curious and contradictory stance towards vegetarianism is the subject of debate.
§ George Bernard Shaw once declined an invitation to a vegetarian gala dinner, stating that 'the thought of two thousand people crunching celery at the same time horrified me'.

## ——— PICCALILLI ———

Piccalilli (known also as mustard pickle, or Indian pickle) is a highly seasoned and slightly spicy vegetable relish. Small pieces of cucumber, beans, onion, cauliflower, marrow (etc.) are brined and mixed with a sauce made from mustard, sugar, white vinegar, and flour. Piccalilli's distinctive yellow hue comes from the inclusion of ginger and turmeric.

## SOME QUOTATIONS ON WINE

CARDINAL RICHELIEU · If God forbade drinking, would He have made wine so good?

UNCLE MONTY · Sherry? Oh dear, no, no, no. I'd be sucked into his trap. One of us has got to stay on guard. He's so mauve. We don't know what he's planning.
[Bruce Robinson, *Withnail and I*]

JOSEPH ADDISON · The Person you converse with, after the third bottle, is not the same Man who first sat down at table with you.

HENRY ARTHUR JONES · Wine is the nurse of all great creative imaginative literature.

THOMAS LOVE PEACOCK · The juice of the grape is the liquid quintessence to concentrated sunbeams.

EURIPIDES · Where there is no wine, love perishes, and everything else that is pleasant to man.

GEORGE HERBERT · Wine is a turncoat: first a friend, than an enemy.

HORACE · Wine brings to light the hidden secrets of the soul.

AMBROSE BIERCE · *Bacchus*: A convenient deity invented by the ancients as an excuse for getting drunk.

JOHN FLETCHER · Be merry, and drink wine that's old, A hearty medicine 'gainst the cold.

GRIMOD DE LA REYNIÈRE · New wine, a friend's dinner, and the music of amateurs are three things to be feared.

OVID · Wine gives courage and makes men apt for passion.

WITHNAIL · Balls. We want the finest wines available to humanity. And we want them *here*. And we want them *now*.     [Bruce Robinson]

## SURSTRÖMMING

The Swedish dish *Surströmming* is a somewhat acquired taste. Small, freshly caught herrings *(strömming)* are placed in wooden vats and a solution of brine is added. After 48 hours or so the heads and intestines are removed and the fish are again packed into barrels with brine. The barrels are left for 8–12 weeks in the summer heat, 'cooking' them at a temperature of 40–60ºF. During this time the fish decompose producing a tremendous quantity of vile pungent gas. The resulting 'delicacy' smells very, very bad indeed, but is regarded by a significant minority as a true gastronomic treat. Sweden's medieval royal legislation, which governs the manufacture of *Surströmming*, allows for its sale on the third Thursday in August, when the fish is traditionally eaten with beer, aquavit, or vodka.

## —— STRAWBERRIES, CREAM, AND ETON MESS ——

It seems frivolous to attempt to surpass the traditional combination of strawberries and cream, however some have tried. The Spanish often moisten strawberries with the juice and zest of oranges, and others use lemon juice, kirsch, or freshly ground pepper. Louis XIV felt that cream was too effeminate an accompaniment and ate his strawberries with wine. (Thomas Hyall wrote in 1592 that this practice was common in England, where strawberries were 'much eaten at all men's tables ... with wine and sugar'.) Certain aficionados employ a fork to mash their strawberries before eating: apparently a Cambridge tradition now practised in Oxford.

Eton Mess is the dessert once traditionally served at the school. It is very simple to make: macerate chopped strawberries in Kirsch and mix them inelegantly with whipped cream and crushed meringue. Serve with strawberries and mint sprigs. (Bananas can be switched for strawberries; both Kirsch and meringue are optional.)

## —— AMERICAN DINER SLANG ——

| | | | |
|---|---|---|---|
| Adam 'n' Eve | two poached eggs | gravel train | sugar bowl |
| murphy | potatoes | haemorrhage | ketchup |
| splash of red | tomato soup | sea dust | salt |
| Adam's ale | water | yum-yum | sugar |
| wreck 'em | scramble the eggs | in the alley | serve as a side dish |
| moo juice | milk | java, joe | coffee |
| belch water | soda water | life-preserver | doughnut |
| on wheels | take-away | breath | onions |
| bucket of hail | glass of ice | looseners | prunes |

| | |
|---|---|
| hounds on an island | sausages on beans |
| put out the lights and cry | liver and onions |
| bucket of cold mud | portion of chocolate ice-cream |
| shingles with a shimmy | toast and jam |
| two cows, make them cry | two hamburgers with onions |
| zeppelins in a fog | sausages in mashed potatoes |

| | | | |
|---|---|---|---|
| burn the British | toasted muffin | lumber | a toothpick |
| clean up the kitchen | hash | mike and 'ike | salt and pepper |
| on a raft | on toast | no cow | without milk |
| wreath | cabbage | sand | sugar |
| bridge | four of anything | a squeeze | orange juice |
| hold the hail | no ice | side-arms | salt and pepper |
| crowd | two of anything | warts | olives |
| Eve with a lid on | apple pie | axle grease | butter |

## CARÊME ON APPETITE

The reported exchange which took place between the Prince Regent (later to become George IV) and his celebrated French cook Antonin Carême:

PRINCE REGENT:
Carême, you will make me die of indigestion. I want to eat everything you send to the table, and the temptation is too great – *en vérité*.

ANTONIN CARÊME:
Sir, my business is to provoke your appetite;
it is not for me to regulate it.

## THE ORTOLAN & PRESIDENT MITTERRAND

The ortolan (or bunting as it is known in England) is a tiny bird no larger than 15cm (3 inches) from tail to beak. The bird features in the work of Colette, Fielding, and Proust, and has a number of effusive advocates:

the flesh is tender, delicate and succulent and the taste is exquisite
AUGUST ESCOFFIER

an epicurean ecstasy … the *transcendentalism* of gastronomy
ALEXIS SOYER

happy is the palate that engulfs it
GRIMOD DE LA REYNIÈRE

In France it is illegal to hunt, buy, or eat ortolans – ordinances which are routinely flouted, most famously by the proud Socialist President Françoise Mitterrand who ate ortolan at his last ever meal. Suffering from end-stage cancer of the prostate, Mitterrand anticipated his imminent death and planned a final banquet. On 31 December 1995, four dishes were served to the President and his guests: Marennes oysters, foie gras, roast capon, and ortolan. The traditional method of preparing and eating ortolan is as curious as it is barbaric. The tiny birds are caught alive and kept in a dark box (or blinded) so that they gorge themselves continuously on grain. Once distended to way beyond their natural size the birds are drowned in Cognac, plucked, and roasted. After their heads have been cut or bitten off, ortolans are eaten whole (bones and all) from underneath a napkin – to hide the shame of such cruelty and gluttony from the sight of God. It is usually considered excessive to eat more than one ortolan, but on the night of his last meal the dying President ate a second – supposedly the last food to pass his lips before he died a week later.

# VEGETARIAN DIETS

Since diets are highly personal, the list below is best understood as giving general descriptions rather than strict definitions. For example, while some totally exclude a foodstuff, others might simply attempt to avoid it.

VEGETARIAN · a vague, catch-all term, usually used to describe someone who excludes meat.

LACTO-VEGETARIAN · excludes all animal products except dairy products.

LACTO-OVO-VEGETARIAN · excludes all animal products except dairy products and eggs.

OVO-VEGETARIAN · excludes all animal products except eggs.

RAW FOODIST · eats fruits, vegetables, nuts, seeds, and soaked and sprouted grains and legumes. Raw foodists tend not to cook food but instead eat it in its raw state to preserve enzymes.

VEGAN · sometimes considered a 'strict' vegetarian, excludes all food which involves the death of an animal. Many exclude honey, sugar and gelatin; some avoid using leather, wool, silk, and the like.

MACROBIOTIC · a vegan diet focusing on lightly cooked grains and vegetables – ideally grown locally and eaten when in season.

FRUITARIAN · excludes all food except raw fruit, grains, and nuts; some will eat plants which can be picked without killing the host (e.g. cucumbers, tomatoes, and avocados, but not carrots).

PESCETARIAN · a vegetarian who consumes fish and shellfish.

# THE TEMPERAMENT OF COOKS

It should also be remembered that an ill-tempered man can never succeed as a master in the culinary art, since the derangement of his gastric juices destroys the peculiar excellence which should govern his palate: it leaves it vitiated and tasteless.

— Charles Pierce, *The Household Manager*, 1863

# CAFFEINATED DRINKS

| *Drink* | *caffeine (mg)* |
|---|---|
| Filter coffee (6fl.oz) | 105 |
| Instant coffee (1 tsp · 6fl.oz) | 60 |
| Decaff coffee (6fl.oz) | 2 |
| Tea (6fl.oz) | 35 |
| Cola (12fl.oz) | 40–50 |
| Decaffeinated cola (12fl.oz) | trace |
| Hot chocolate (6fl.oz) | 4 |

**E-Number Groupings**

| | |
|---|---|
| 100–199 | food colours |
| 200–299 | preservatives |
| 300–399 | antioxidants, phosphates, and complexing agents |
| 400–499 | thickeners, gelling agents, phosphates, emulsifiers |
| 500–599 | salts and related compounds |
| 600–699 | flavour enhancers |
| 700–899 | *not for human food additives* |
| 900–999 | surface-coating agents, gases, sweeteners |
| 1000–1399 | miscellaneous |
| 1400–1499 | starch derivatives |

**List of E-Numbers**

| | |
|---|---|
| E100 | Curcumin |
| E101 | Riboflavins |
| E102 | Tartrazine |
| E104 | Quinoline Yellow |
| E110 | Sunset Yellow, Orange Yellow S |
| E120 | Cochineal, Carminic acid, Carmines |
| E122 | Azorubin, Carmoisine |
| E123 | Amaranth |
| E124 | Ponceau 4R, Cochineal Red A |
| E127 | Erythrosine |
| E128 | Red 2G |
| E129 | Allura Red AC |
| E131 | Patent Blue V |
| E132 | Indigotine, Indigo Carmine |
| E133 | Brilliant Blue FCF |
| E140 | Chlorophylls and chlorophyllins |
| E141 | Copper complexes of chlorophylls and chlorophyllins |
| E142 | Green S |
| E150a | Plain caramel |
| E150b | Caustic sulphite caramel |
| E150c | Ammonia caramel |
| E150d | Sulphite ammonia caramel |
| E151 | Brilliant Black BN, Black BN |
| E153 | Vegetable carbon |
| E154 | Brown FK |
| E155 | Brown HT |
| E160a | Carotenes |
| E160b | Anatto, bixin, norbixin |
| E160c | Paprika extract, capsanthin, capsorubin |
| E160d | Lycopene |
| E160e | Beta-apo-8'-carotenal (C 30) |
| E160f | Ethyl ester of Beta-apo-8'-carotenic acid (C30) |
| E161b | Lutein |
| E161g | Canthaxanthin |
| E162 | Beetroot Red, betanin |
| E163 | Anthocyanins |
| E170 | Calcium carbonates |
| E171 | Titanium dioxide |
| E172 | Iron oxides and hydroxides |
| E173 | Aluminum |
| E174 | Silver |
| E175 | Gold |
| E180 | Litholrubine BK |
| E200 | Sorbic acid |
| E202 | Potassium sorbate |
| E203 | Calcium sorbate |
| E210 | Benzoic acid |
| E211 | Sodium benzoate |
| E212 | Potassium benzoate |
| E213 | Calcium benzoate |
| E214 | Ethyl p-hydroxybenzoate |
| E215 | Sodium ethyl p-hydroxybenzoate |
| E216 | Propyl p-hydroxybenzoate |
| E217 | Sodium propyl p-hydroxybenzoate |
| E218 | Methyl p-hydroxybenzoate |
| E219 | Sodium methyl p-hydroxybenzoate |
| E220 | Sulphur dioxide |
| E221 | Sodium sulphite |
| E222 | Sodium hydrogen sulphite |
| E223 | Sodium metabisulphite |
| E224 | Potassium metabisulphite |
| E226 | Calcium sulphite |
| E227 | Calcium hydrogen sulphite |
| E228 | Potassium hydrogen sulphite |
| E230 | Biphenyl, diphenyl |
| E231 | Orthophenyl phenol |
| E232 | Sodium orthophenyl phenol |
| E233 | Thiabendazole |
| E234 | Nisin |
| E235 | Natamycin |
| E239 | Hexamethylene tetramine |
| E242 | Dimethyl dicarbonate |
| E249 | Potassium nitrite |
| E250 | Sodium nitrite |
| E251 | Sodium nitrate |
| E252 | Potassium nitrate |
| E260 | Acetic acid |
| E261 | Potassium acetate |
| E262 | Sodium acetates |
| E263 | Calcium acetate |
| E270 | Lactic acid |
| E280 | Propionic acid |
| E281 | Sodium propionate |
| E282 | Calcium propionate |
| E283 | Potassium propionate |
| E284 | Boric acid |
| E285 | Sodium tetraborate (borax) |
| E290 | Carbon dioxide |
| E296 | Malic acid |
| E297 | Fumaric acid |
| E300 | Ascorbic acid |
| E301 | Sodium ascorbate |
| E302 | Calcium ascorbate |
| E304 | Fatty acid esters of ascorbic acid |
| E306 | Tocopherol-rich extract |
| E307 | Alpha – tocopherol |
| E308 | Gamma – tocopherol |
| E309 | Delta – tocopherol |
| E310 | Propyl gallate |
| E311 | Octyl gallate |
| E312 | Dodecyl gallate |
| E315 | Erythorbic acid |
| E316 | Sodium erythorbate |
| E320 | Butylated hydroxyanisole (BHA) |
| E321 | Butylated hydroxytoluene (BHT) |
| E322 | Lecithins |
| E325 | Sodium lactate |
| E326 | Potassium lactate |
| E327 | Calcium lactate |
| E330 | Citric acid |
| E331 | Sodium citrates |
| E332 | Potassium citrates |
| E333 | Calcium citrates |
| E334 | Tartaric acid (L(+)-) |
| E335 | Sodium tartrates |
| E336 | Potassium tartrates |
| E337 | Sodium potassium tartrate |
| E338 | Phosphoric acid |
| E339 | Sodium phosphates |
| E340 | Potassium phosphates |
| E341 | Calcium phosphates |
| E343 | Magnesium phosphates |
| E350 | Sodium malates |
| E351 | Potassium malate |
| E352 | Calcium malates |
| E353 | Metatartaric acid |
| E354 | Calcium tartrate |
| E355 | Adipic acid |
| E356 | Sodium adipate |
| E357 | Potassium adipate |
| E363 | Succinic acid |
| E380 | Triammonium citrate |
| E385 | Calcium disodium ethylene diamine tetra-acetate |
| E400 | Alginic acid |
| E401 | Sodium alginate |
| E402 | Potassium alginate |
| E403 | Ammonium alginate |
| E404 | Calcium alginate |
| E405 | Propane-1,2-diol alginate |
| E406 | Agar |
| E407 | Carrageenan |
| E407a | Processed eucheuma seaweed |
| E410 | Locust bean gum |
| E412 | Guar gum |
| E413 | Tragacanth |
| E414 | Acacia gum (gum arabic) |
| E415 | Xanthan gum |
| E416 | Karaya gum |
| E417 | Tara gum |
| E418 | Gellan gum |
| E420 | Sorbitol |
| E421 | Mannitol |
| E422 | Glycerol |
| E425 | Konjac |

E431 ... Polyoxyethylene (40) stearate
E432 ... Polyoxyethylene sorbitan monolaurate (polysorbate 20)
E433 ... Polyoxyethylene sorbitan monooleate (polysorbate 80)
E434 ... Polyoxyethylene sorbitan monopalmitate (polysorbate 40)
E435 ... Polyoxyethylene sorbitan monostearate (polysorbate 60)
E436 ... Polyoxyethylene sorbitan tristearate (polysorbate 65)
E440 ... Pectins
E442 ... Ammonium phosphatides
E444 ... Sucrose acetate isobutyrate
E445 ... Glycerol esters of wood rosin
E450 ... Diphosphates
E451 ... Triphosphates
E452 ... Polyphosphates
E459 ... Beta-Cyclodextrine
E460 ... Cellulose
E461 ... Methylcellulose
E463 ... Hydroxypropyl cellulose
E464 ... Hydroxypropyl methyl cellulose
E465 ... Ethyl methyl cellulose
E466 ... Carboxy methyl cellulose
E468 ... Crosslinked sodium carboxy methyl cellulose
E469 ... Enzymatically hydrolysed carboxy methyl cellulose
E470a ... Sodium, potassium and calcium salts of fatty acids
E470b ... Magnesium salts of fatty acids
E471 ... Mono & diglycerides of fatty acids
E472a ... Acetic acid esters of mono and diglycerides of fatty acids
E472b ... Lactic acid esters of mono and diglycerides of fatty acids
E472c ... Citric acid esters of mono and diglycerides of fatty acids
E472d ... Tartaric acid esters of mono and diglycerides of fatty acids
E472e ... Mono & diacetyl tartaric acid esters of mono & diglycerides of fatty acids

E472f ... Mixed acetic & tartaric acid ester of mono and diglycerides of fatty acids
E473 ... Sucrose esters of fatty acids
E474 ... Sucroglycerides
E475 ... Polyglycerol esters of fatty acids
E476 ... Polyglycerol polyricinoleate
E477 ... Propan-1,2-diol esters of fatty acids
E479b ... Thermally oxidized soya bean oil
E481 ... Sodium stearoyl-2-lactylate
E482 ... Calcium stearoyl-2-lactylate
E483 ... Stearyl tartrate
E491 ... Sorbitan monostearate
E492 ... Sorbitan tristearate
E493 ... Sorbitan monolaurate
E494 ... Sorbitan monooleate
E495 ... Sorbitan monopalmitate
E500 ... Sodium carbonates
E501 ... Potassium carbonates
E503 ... Ammonium carbonates
E504 ... Magnesium carbonates
E507 ... Hydrochloric acid
E508 ... Potassium chloride
E509 ... Calcium chloride
E511 ... Magnesium chloride
E512 ... Stannous chloride
E513 ... Sulphuric acid
E514 ... Sodium sulphates
E515 ... Potassium sulphates
E516 ... Calcium sulphate
E517 ... Ammonium sulphate
E520 ... Aluminium sulphate
E521 ... Aluminium sodium sulphate
E522 ... Aluminium potassium sulphate
E523 ... Aluminium ammonium sulphate
E524 ... Sodium hydroxide
E525 ... Potassium hydroxide
E526 ... Calcium hydroxide
E527 ... Ammonium hydroxide
E528 ... Magnesium hydroxide
E529 ... Calcium oxide
E530 ... Magnesium oxide
E535 ... Sodium ferrocyanide
E536 ... Potassium ferrocyanide

E538 ... Calcium ferrocyanide
E541 ... Sodium aluminium phosphate, acidic
E551 ... Silicon dioxide
E552 ... Calcium silicate
E553a ... Magnesium silicates
E553b ... Talc
E554 ... Sodium aluminium silicate
E555 ... Potassium aluminium silicate
E556 ... Calcium aluminium silicate
E558 ... Bentonite
E559 ... Aluminium silicate (Kaolin)
E570 ... Fatty acids
E574 ... Gluconic acid
E575 ... Glucono-delta-lactone
E576 ... Sodium gluconate
E577 ... Potassium gluconate
E578 ... Calcium gluconate
E579 ... Ferrous gluconate
E585 ... Ferrous lactate
E620 ... Glutamic acid
E621 ... Monosodium glutamate
E622 ... Monopotassium glutamate
E623 ... Calcium diglutamate
E624 ... Monoammonium glutamate
E625 ... Magnesium diglutamate
E626 ... Guanylic acid
E627 ... Disodium guanylate
E628 ... Dipotassium guanylate
E629 ... Calcium guanylate
E630 ... Inosinic acid
E631 ... Disodium inosinate
E632 ... Dipotassium inosinate
E633 ... Calcium inosinate
E634 ... Calcium 5'-ribonucleotides
E635 ... Disodium 5'-ribonucleotides
E640 ... Glycine and its sodium salt
E650 ... Zinc Acetate
E900 ... Dimethyl polysiloxane
E901 ... Bees wax, white and yellow
E902 ... Candelilla wax
E903 ... Carnauba wax
E904 ... Shellac
E905 ... Microcrystalline wax

E912 ... Montan acid esters
E914 ... Oxidized polyethylene wax
E920 ... L-Cysteine
E927b ... Carbamide
E938 ... Argon
E939 ... Helium
E941 ... Nitrogen
E942 ... Nitrous oxide
E943a ... Butane
E943b ... Iso-Butane
E944 ... Propane
E948 ... Oxygen
E949 ... Hydrogen
E950 ... Acesulfame-K
E951 ... Aspartame
E952 ... Cyclamic acid & its Na & Ca salts
E953 ... Isomalt
E954 ... Saccharin & its Na, K & Ca salts
E957 ... Thaumatin
E959 ... Neohesperidine DC
E965 ... Maltitol
E966 ... Lactitol
E967 ... Xylitol
E999 ... Quillaia extract
E1103 ... Invertase
E1105 ... Lysozyme
E1200 ... Polydextrose
E1201 ... Polyvinylpyrrolidone
E1202 ... Polyvinylpolypyrrolidone
E1404 ... Oxidized starch
E1410 ... Monostarch phosphate
E1412 ... Distarch phosphate
E1413 ... Phosphated distarch phosphate
E1414 ... Acetylated distarch phosphate
E1420 ... Acetylated starch
E1422 ... Acetylated distarch adipate
E1440 ... Hydroxy propyl starch
E1442 ... Hydroxy propyl distarch phosphate
E1450 ... Starch sodium octenyl succinate
E1451 ... Acetylated oxidized starch
E1505 ... Triethyl citrate
E1518 ... Glyceryl triacetate (triacetin)
E1520 ... Propylene glycol

——————————— BAGELS ———————————

Bagels (*beygls* in Yiddish) are ring-shaped buns with a dense chewy texture (from being poached in boiling water) and a crisp glossy finish (from being brushed with egg-yolk). They are one of the traditional Jewish breads – possibly invented in 1683 by a Viennese baker, but certainly popularised in the Polish *shtetl*. According to the legendary food-writer Claudia Roden 'because of their shape – with no beginning and no end – bagels symbolise the eternal cycle of life. In the old days they were supposed to be a protection against demons and evil spirits, warding off the evil eye and bringing good luck. For these reasons they were served at circumcisions and when a woman was in labour and also at funerals...'

——————————— FRENCH FOOD TIMING ———————————

*Oeuf d'une heure; pain d'un jour; vin d'un an*
Eggs an hour old; bread a day old; wine a year old

——————————— BRISTOL STOOL FORM CHART ———————————

Devised by K. Heaton et al. in 1992, the Bristol Stool Form Chart aims to assist medical diagnosis by categorising bowel movements into 7 types:

| | | |
|---|---|---|
| 1 | Separate hard lumps, like nuts | 1 |
| 2 | Sausage-shaped, but lumpy | 2 |
| 3 | Like a sausage or snake but with cracks on its surface | 3 |
| 4 | Like a sausage or snake, smooth and soft | 4 |
| 5 | Soft blobs with clear-cut edges | 5 |
| 6 | Fluffy pieces with ragged edges, a mushy stool | 6 |
| 7 | Water, no solid pieces | 7 |

*Healthy stools are usually considered to be those falling into categories 3 or 4.*

——————————— STIR-UP SUNDAY ———————————

The Sunday before Advent is Stir-Up Sunday – the last day that cakes and puddings could be started if they were to be ready before Christmas. Curiously, the day is named not after the act of stirring, but after the Collect used on that day: 'Stir up we beseech thee, O Lord, the will of thy faithful people...' Notwithstanding this etymology, there is a long tradition of rituals for stirring Christmas puddings. At University College Junior School, London, for example, the youngest boy was given the privilege of stirring the pudding-mix in front of the assembled school.

--------- SALT ---------

❧ Salt is the common term for *sodium chloride* (NaCl). It is one of the basic *tastes* (see p.23), and is an essential component of a healthy diet (see p.89). ❧ Salt has long been used as a *preservative* for meat and vegetables, yet salt also *corrodes* materials such as metal. ❧ The Greek biographer *Plutarch* called salt the 'noblest of foods, the finest condiment of all'. ❧ To the *Ancient Greeks* and the *Children of Israel* salt was a symbol of hospitality and union, as it is to *Muslims* today. In *Arab* tradition, to *eat a man's salt* is to take his hospitality, an act which implies an enduring bond of loyalty. The *Russian* term for hospitality – *khleb-sol'* – translates literally as bread-salt. ❧ In *alchemical* terms, salt is considered to derive from all four *elements: 'fire* freed from the *waters* of the *earth* by *evaporation'*. ❧ *Spilling* salt has long been considered unlucky by the superstitious, who maintain that once salt is spilled, bad fortune may by averted by throwing a pinch of it over the left shoulder with one's right hand. Ominously, Leonardo's *Last Supper* depicts *Judas* as having knocked over a salt-cellar by his elbow (see p.116). It is claimed that in 1716 the *Marquis de Montrevel*, a French marshal noted for his courage, was so horrified when a salt-cellar was spilled over him, he died of fright. ❧ Christ's Apostles were likened to *'the salt of the earth'* [Matthew 5:13], and the Bible makes a number of references to salt symbolising *incorruptibility* – hence a *covenant of salt* is one which cannot be broken [2 Chronicles 13:5]. ❧ The word *salary* is derived from the Latin for salt *(salarium)*, which was the money given to Roman soldiers to buy salt. (Indeed, *soldier* derives from the French for salt, *sol.*) Thus, to be *true to one's salt* is to be faithful to one's employers. ❧ A host of armies have *salted the earth* to make the soil barren and deny their enemies a harvest. (Odysseus, in an attempt to avoid fighting in the Trojan Wars, feigned madness by *ploughing his fields* with salt.) ❧ In the *Shinto* religion salt plays a role in ceremonies such as *funerals*, and it is considered to have *cleansing* powers – hence salt is often placed in small mounds next to wells or by the entrance to houses. ❧ To *Shakespeare*, salt symbolised youth and vigour, and he employed it as a metaphor for *sexual passion* [e.g. Othello III.iii]. ❧ Venerable sailors are known as *'old salts'* or *'salty sea-dogs'* – and the metaphorical idea of *rubbing salt into a wound* derives from the nautical practice of applying salt to the lacerations after a *flogging*. ❧ Formal *dining tables* had an ornate *saler* (salt-cellar) placed half-way down their length. Since anyone of any rank would sit towards the head of the table, above the *saler*, the expression *below the salt* came to be used. ❧ Under British rule, salt in *India* was controlled by state monopoly and heavily taxed. In 1930, at a beach in Dandi, *Mahatma Gandhi* symbolically broke the law by picking up a handful of sea-salt. This simple act catalysed a wave of public protest which forced the Viceroy, Lord Irwin, into negotiations. ❧ *Satan* is said to hate salt, which explains the phrase 'the Devil serves a saltless meal' as well as the superstition of throwing salt over a *coffin.* ❧

## LAOTIAN COOKING MEASURES

| Western equivalent | Laoation term | Rough Metric |
|---|---|---|
| soupspoonful | *tem buang ken* | 10ml |
| spoonful | *tem buang* | 15ml |
| hen's egg | *khai kai* | 45ml |
| ladleful | *jong* | 100–285ml |
| ricebowl | *tauy mak toom* | 140ml |
| beaker | *jawk* | 285ml |
| jug | *jok* | 570ml |

## SHROVE TUESDAY & THE DORCHESTER

Shrove Tuesday (Pancake Day) precedes Ash Wednesday and the period of Lenten fasting. Pancakes were eaten to use up proscribed foods, and it is claimed that their ingredients have special Lenten symbolism: flour is the staff of life; milk is innocence and purity; salt is incorruptibility; and eggs symbolise creation. Below are some gourmet Shrove Tuesday pancakes taken from the archives of the Dorchester Hotel, London:

### DORSET DROP
Filled with apple and currants, passed through coconut and deep fried, served with clotted cream and a light English custard cream

### ST. CLEMENTS
Filled with oranges and lemons, rolled dusted with sugar and served with sweetened cream

### DORCHESTER
Filled with sliced pears, rolled, coated with creamed pear liqueur sauce and browned in a hot oven

### MARJORIE
Filled with soufflé cream, peaches, folded and baked in the oven served with a light sauce

### SEAFARER
Filled with vanilla ice-cream and coated with a light rum caramel sauce

## BANQUETING LEGISLATION

In 1517 a royal proclamation was issued in an attempt to curb excessive feasting. The number of dishes which could be served was regulated 'according to the rank of the highest person present'. Thus if the host, or one of the guests, was a CARDINAL, nine courses could legally be served; if a LORD OF PARLIAMENT, six courses; and if a CITIZEN with an income of £500 per year, three courses. (In 1336 a law to limit 'extravagant expenses in diet' forbade anyone from eating more than two courses.)

## —BRILLAT-SAVARIN'S GASTRONOMIC TESTS—

Culinary philosopher Jean-Anthelme Brillat-Savarin (1755–1826) boldly asserted that gastronomes formed a special class, uniquely able to perceive and savour the pleasures of taste. True gastronomes, he claimed, could be distinguished by their response to certain foods – the mere sight of which would arouse gustatory ecstasy in a 'believer'. To separate the gastronome from the unworthy masses, Brillat-Savarin devised three test menus:

### —— FIRST MENU ——

*Presumed income of 5,000 Francs (mediocrity)*

A large fillet of veal, larded with bacon and cooked in its own juices · Country-fed turkey, stuffed with chestnuts · Fattened pigeons, larded and cooked · Eggs à la neige · Sauerkraut, with sausages and the finest bacon

*Expression: 'By golly! That looks all right. Come on! Let us do it justice!'*

### —— SECOND MENU ——

*Presumed income of 15,000 Francs (comfort)*

The choicest fillet of beef, well larded and cooked in its own juices · Haunch of venison with gherkin sauce · A boiled turbot · Leg of pré-salé mutton served à la Provençale · Turkey stuffed with truffles · Early green peas

*Expression: 'My dear friend, what a delightful sight. This truly is a feast.'*

### —— THIRD MENU ——

*Presumed income of 30,000 Francs or more (riches)*

A 7lb fowl stuffed to repletion with Périgord truffles · A Strasbourg pâté de foie gras, shaped as a bastion · A large Rhine carp richly dressed · Truffled quails with marrow served on basil-flavoured buttered toast · A stuffed and larded pike, with prawn sauce secundum artem · Pheasant larded en toupet, à la Saint-Alliance · 100 early asparagus à l'Osmazôme · 24 ortolans à la Provençale · Meringue cake

*'Ah, Monsieur (or My Lord), what a genius your cook must be! One only eats such dishes at your table.'*

Each menu was aimed at a different class, since a financier would hardly be challenged by that which could challenge a humble clerk. By carefully studying the responses elicited by each course (which become increasingly elaborate) the gastronomic credentials of an individual could be verified.

---

## PICA

---

Pica is a little-understood eating disorder usually defined as the ingestion of non-nutritional, non-food items, often in a compulsive manner.[†] To the general public pica is most commonly associated with pregnant women, who occasionally suffer cravings for bizarre non-foods like earth, coal, soap, or clay. However, medics also observe pica in other groups, including young children and the mentally ill. The causes of this disorder remain uncertain – though it seems that some curious cravings during pregnancy may be linked to abnormal levels of iron. When categorising eating disorders, medics employ a host of terms describing consumption of abnormal things and the mechanical problems related to eating:

NON-FOOD CONSUMPTION

| | |
|---|---|
| Amylophagia | *starch* |
| Cautopyreiophagia | *burnt matches* |
| Coprophagia | *faeces* |
| Geomelophagia | *raw potatoes* |
| Geophagia | *dry earth, clay* |
| Hyalophagia | *glass* |
| Lithophagia | *stones* |
| Monophagia | *one food only* |
| Pagophagia | *ice* |

| | |
|---|---|
| Plumbophagia | *lead (paint chips)* |
| Trichophagia | *hair* |

MECHANICAL DISORDERS

| | |
|---|---|
| Aerophagia | *swallowing excess air* |
| Bradyphagia | *abnormal slowness* |
| Dysphagia | *difficulty in swallowing* |
| Odynophagia | *pain on swallowing* |
| Polyphagia | *excessive eating* |
| Sialophagia | *swallowing excess saliva* |

† The term derives from the Latin for magpie, *pica* – a bird notorious for its scavenging.

---

## OSTRICH EGGS

---

1 ostrich egg is equivalent to 24 hen's eggs. The Khoikhoi would place an egg on hot ashes, pierce the shell and stir the contents into an omelette.

---

## CHOCOLATE FACTORY CHILDREN

---

In Roald Dahl's timeless classic *Charlie and the Chocolate Factory* (1964), five lucky children find the golden tickets which secure them entry into Willy Wonka's chocolate factory. All but the hero, Charlie Bucket, come to unfortunate and sticky ends through their spoilt and greedy behaviour:

| | |
|---|---|
| Augustus Gloop | *falls into the chocolate river and is sucked up a tube* |
| Violet Beauregarde | *turned into a blueberry by eating chewing gum* |
| Veruca Salt | *attacked by walnut-shelling squirrels* |
| Mike Teavee | *shrunk by the Television Chocolate camera* |

———————————— CAVIAR ————————————

Originating from the Turkish word *khavia* – caviar consists of the salted eggs of various species of sturgeon. (The Russian term is *ikra*.) Fastidious eaters assert that the best caviar originates from the Caspian Sea and that three species of sturgeon produce the finest eggs, listed here in price order:

| *Name* (species) | *Eggs per gram* | *Colouring* |
|---|---|---|
| BELUGA *(Acipenser huso)* | 30 | pale to dark grey |
| OSIETRA *(Acipenser guldenstaedti)* | 50 | grey to golden brown |
| SEVRUGA *(Acipenser stellatus)* | 70 | dark grey to black |

Caviar was introduced to France in the 1920s by two Russian brothers, Melkom and Mougcheg Petrossian, who were astonished to find that the delicacy so popular in their homeland had not found a following in Paris, the gastronomic capital of the world. Yet when the brothers held caviar tastings at the 1925 Universal Exhibition in the Grand Palais, they were compelled to provide spitoons to cater for the public's initial reaction.

———————————— ASKING FOR THE BILL ————————————

| | |
|---|---|
| Arabic | *al-Hisaab, low samaht* |
| Bavarian | *Tsoin!* |
| Bulgarian | *molya, smetkata* |
| Chinese | *Qing jié zhàng ba* |
| Czech | Prosim ucet |
| Dutch | De rekening, alstublieft |
| Estonian | Palun arve |
| Finnish | Haluaisin maksaa |
| French | L'addition, s'il vous plaît |
| German | Die Rechnung, bitte |
| Greek | *toh logaree-azmo, parakalo* |
| Hebrew | *efshar lekabel et ha-kheshbon, bevakasar* |
| Italian | Il conto, per favore |
| Japanese | *o-kanjoo onegai shimasu* |
| Latvian | ludzu rekinu |
| Morse code | – .... / –... .– ..–.. .–... / – .– ... |
| Polish | Poprosze rachunek |
| Portuguese | A conta, por favor |
| Serbo-Croatian | Racun, molim |
| Spanish | La cuenta, por favor |
| Swahili | Unaweza kunipa jumla ya hesabu? |
| Turkish | Hesabi, lüften |

*Not forgetting the international code of signing your name in the air. (Italics = phonetics)*

## THE HARRIS-BENEDICT EQUATION

The Harris-Benedict equation is one of a number of formulas employed to calculate the Resting Energy Expenditure (REE) in Calories per day:

Female REE (Calories/day) =
$$655 + (9{\cdot}5 \times \text{weight in kg}) + (1{\cdot}9 \times \text{height in cm}) - (4{\cdot}7 \times \text{age in years})$$

Male REE (Calories/day) =
$$66 + (13{\cdot}8 \times \text{weight in kg}) + (5{\cdot}0 \times \text{height in cm}) - (6{\cdot}8 \times \text{age in years})$$

The REE represents the Calories required in 24 hours of relative inactivity.

## FUGU & JAPANESE FUGU CHEFS

*Fugu* is the Japanese term for certain species of blowfish, of which the most popular are *Fugu rubripes* (torafugu) and *Fugu porphyreus* (mafugu). The fish has received international notoriety because its gut, liver, ovaries, and skin contain tetrodotoxin – a poison over 1,000 times more potent than cyanide. Although not necessarily fatal (there is a 40% chance of survival), tetrodotoxin acts within minutes to block the sodium channels of certain tissues, causing weakness, nausea, sweating, diarrhoea, and tingling. In serious cases convulsions set in and paralysis restricts breathing. When fatal, *fugu* causes complete respiratory failure sometimes within an hour. A number of unfortunate or foolhardy diners die each year after eating the fish. Perhaps the most famous victim of *fugu* was the Japanese kabuki actor Mitsugoro Bando VIII, who died in 1975 after eating four servings of *fugu* liver. However, it has been suggested that in 1774 Captain James Cook may have experienced the mild side-effects of *fugu* poisoning while in New Caledonia. *Fugu* has also entered the world of fiction, most notably in Ian Fleming's James Bond novels. *From Russia With Love* ends just as Bond has been stabbed by the SMERSH henchman Rosa Klebb, who had concealed a poisoned blade in her shoe. We later learn, in *Dr No*, that the poison was tetrodotoxin from *fugu*; as Sir James Molony tells M, *'trust the Russians to use something no one's ever heard of'*.

Japanese *fugu* chefs are strictly licensed by the government. In the Tokyo prefecture, for example, a *fugu*-chef exam is held every August, for which applicants must be over 18, have no criminal record, have good eyesight (glasses are permitted), and have spent at least two years apprenticed to a licensed *fugu* chef. The exam costs ¥17,900 (*c.*£100), and is in two parts: a written test on *fugu* and Tokyo's *fugu* regulations; and a practical test to identify five different types of fugu, separate the *fugu*'s poisonous glands, and prepare three *fugu* dishes – chiri, kawahiki, and sashimi. Chefs forfeit their licence if they sell illegal fish, handle fugu in unrestricted areas, lend their licence to another, or fail to meet the stringent health and safety standards. *Fugu* waste must be kept in a locked container before being burnt.

## RESTAURANT & KITCHEN STAFF

HIERARCHY OF STAFF IN A
MODERN RESTAURANT

Manager
Assistant Manager
Senior Floor Manager
Floor Manager
Head Waiter
Chef de Rang
Demi Chef de Rang
Commis Waiter
Head Sommelier [wine waiter]
Assistant Head Sommelier
Sommelier
Demi Sommelier
Commis Sommelier
———
Executive Head Chef
Head Chef
Senior Sous Chef
Sous Chef
Junior Sous Chef
Senior Chef de Partie
Commis Chef
Chef Apprentice
———
Head Baker
1st Baker
Baker

TRADITIONAL FRENCH
'BRIGADE DE CUISINE'

Chef de Cuisine
Sous Chef
Chef de Partie
Les Garde-mangers [larder chefs]
Boucher [butcher]
Les Sauciers [sauce chefs]
Les Poissoniers [fish chefs]
Les Potages [soup chefs]
Les Entremettiers [vegetable chefs]
Les Rôtisseurs [roast chefs]
Les Brocheurs [spit roasters]
Les Potagers [vegetable chefs]
Les Grillardins [grill chefs]
Les Cocottiers [egg chefs]
Les Frituriers [fryers]
Les Fourniers [oven chefs]
Les Touriers [dough makers]
Les Confiseurs [confectioners]
Les Glaçiers [ice-cream chefs]
Les Pâtissiers [pastry chefs]
Le Chef du Nuit [night cook]
Le Communard [staff chef]
Les Trancheurs [carvers]
L'Apprenti [apprentice]
Aboyeur [kitchen clerk]
Plongeur [dishwasher]

## KOPI LUWAK

Often cited as the most expensive coffee in the world, *Kopi Luwak* is distinguished by its 'fundamental' origin. The common palm civet *(Paradoxurus hermaphrodites)* is a nocturnal tree-living carnivore found on the coffee plantations of south-east Asia. As well as small mammals and insects, the diet of these civets includes fruits and berries – especially the ripest coffee-cherries. It is claimed that, once eaten, these coffee-cherries pass through the digestive system of the civets, emerging not only intact, but somehow 'matured' by the stomach enzymes with which they have come into contact, creating a dark, rich, 'musty' flavour. *Kopi Luwak* is marketed as the 'rarest beverage in the world': it sells for $200 per pound.

## ——— MRS BEETON'S CHRISTMAS PUDDING ———

½lb beef suet · 2oz flour · ½lb raisins
¼lb mixed peel · ½ small grated nutmeg · 1 gill milk
¼oz mixed spice · ¼oz ground cinnamon
1 wineglassful of rum or brandy
½lb breadcrumbs · ½lb sultanas · ½lb currants · 1 lemon
2oz desiccated coconut · 4 eggs · 1 pinch of salt

METHOD: Shred the suet, or use packet shredded. Clean the fruit, stone the raisins, finely shred the mixed peel; peel and chop the lemon rind. Put all the dry ingredients in a basin and mix well. Add the milk, stir the eggs one at a time, add the rum or brandy and the strained juice of the lemon. Work the whole thoroughly for some minutes, so that the ingredients are well blended. Put the mixture in a well-greased basin or a greased or floured pudding cloth. TIME: Boil for about 4 hours, or steam for at least 5 hours. Sufficient for 8–9 persons. *(Flame with warm cognac or brandy.)*

## ——— UK CHOCOLATE LABELLING DEFINITIONS ———

'CHOCOLATE' must contain
≥35% total dry cocoa solids including
≥18% cocoa butter and ≥14% dry non-fat cocoa solids

'MILK CHOCOLATE' must contain
≥25% dry cocoa solids; ≥14% dry milk solids;
≥2·5% dry non-fat cocoa solids; ≥3·5% milk fat; ≥25% total fat

## ——— SOME BREADS OF THE WORLD ———

Almost every culture has a number of characteristic breads – made distinct by their ingredients, shape, cooking methods, or by a particular ceremony with which they are associated. For example: Italian *focaccia, ciabatta, biova, panettone,* and *pagnotta;* Swiss *bauerruch, birnbrot, bangeli,* and *Vogel loaf;* Danish *julekage,* and *fasterlavnsboiller;* Finnish *halkaka* and *rieska;* Portuguese *rosquilha,* and *broa de milho;* German *pumpernickel, landbrot,* and *mandelbrot;* Spanish *pan cateto, hornazo,* and *ensaimada;* Chinese *man to;* Greek *daktyla;* Lebanese *mankoush;* Armenian *pideh;* Jewish *challah, sumsums, matzo,* and *kubaneh;* American *sourdough;* Indian *paratha, chapati, naan, poori,* and *roti;* Australian *damper bread;* Belgian *pistolet;* English *bloomer, hot-cross bun, crumpet, lardy-cake,* and *huffkin;* French *baguette, brioche, pain de campagne, epi,* and *cereale;* Welsh *bara brith;* Irish *soda bread* and *boxty;* Scottish *oatcake,* and *bannock;* etc.

## RUSSIAN-DOLL ROAST

Below is one of many versions of the famous Russian-doll-like roast. Its preparation is complex and laborious (it is wise to debone all of the birds larger than the ortolan), and there is always the vexed question of how long to cook the monster once it is prepared. Eighteen hours of moderate roasting seems a reasonable time, but be sure to check the juices run clear.

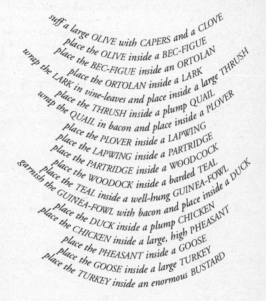

stuff a large OLIVE with CAPERS and a CLOVE
place the OLIVE inside a BEC-FIGUE
place the BEC-FIGUE inside an ORTOLAN
place the ORTOLAN inside a LARK
wrap the LARK in vine-leaves and place inside a large THRUSH
place the THRUSH inside a plump QUAIL
wrap the QUAIL in bacon and place inside a PLOVER
place the PLOVER inside a LAPWING
place the LAPWING inside a PARTRIDGE
place the PARTRIDGE inside a WOODCOCK
place the WOODOCK inside a barded TEAL
garnish the TEAL inside a well-hung GUINEA-FOWL
place the GUINEA-FOWL with bacon and place inside a DUCK
place the DUCK inside a plump CHICKEN
place the CHICKEN inside a large, high PHEASANT
place the PHEASANT inside a GOOSE
place the GOOSE inside a large TURKEY
place the TURKEY inside an enormous BUSTARD

## TERROIR

*Terroir* is the quintessentially French (part geographical, part philosophical) term for the environment, soil, and soul of a vineyard. Definitions are suitably hazy for such a poetical concept, but *terroir* is usually considered to include such factors as soil-type, climate, topography, geology, pedology, hydrology, irrigation, altitude, and position. Many claim that the quality and character of a wine are heavily influenced by the *terroir* of its birth; others argue that preoccupation with *terroir* is little more than superstition. Either way, it seems that advances in wine technology may be diminishing the influence of *terroir*, producing more uniform wines. Some of France's classic wines purportedly grow on the very finest *terroir*, but, then again, similar soil can produce wines barely worth uncorking.

--- POISONOUS MUSHROOMS ---

People have been dying from mushroom poisoning (accidentally or otherwise) since mushrooms have been gathered, and a curious group of notables have died this way including: Pope Clement VII, Emperor Diocletian, and Emperor Karl VII. It is claimed that Euripides lost his wife, two sons, and a daughter to fungi in one day; and, according to Pliny, Emperor Claudius was poisoned with mushrooms by his wife Agrippina. The effects of mushroom poisoning range from mild indigestion, cramp, and nausea, to acute pain, loss of consciousness, and, ultimately, death. The incubation time usually varies from a few hours to some days, although one fungus native to Poland – *Cortinarius (Dermocybe) orellanus* – can take more than two weeks to show its lethal effect. Because of these risks diligent caution should be exercised with all fungi. Below are some of the more deadly fungi always to be avoided:

| DEADLY GALERINA *Galerina autumnalis* | DEATH CAP *Amanita phalloides* | YELLOW STAINER *Agaricus xanthodermus* |
| DESTROYING ANGEL *Amanita virosa* | FLY AGARIC *Amanita muscaria* | LAWN FUNNEL-CAP *Clitocybe dealbata* |

A few species of fungi become more dangerous if eaten in conjunction with alcohol – for example: *Coprinus atramentarius* and *Boletus luridus*.

--- BROSIER ---

In Eton College slang, *brosier* was the ploy of showing contempt for the food served at a house by devouring absolutely everything within reach.
[*The term may derive from a slang C18th term for bankruptcy.*]

## PUNCH

The following is a description of the punch served at a banquet given by Sir Edward Russell, Commander-in-Chief of the British forces, in 1746:

> *The bowl was the marble basin of a delightful garden, forming the central point of four vast avenues, bordered with orange and lemon trees. A magnificent collation was served on four immense tables, which occupied the length of several avenues. The basin had been filled with four large barrels of brandy, eight barrels of filtered water, twenty-five thousand citrons, eighty pints of lemon juice, thirteen hundred weight of sugar, five pounds of nutmeg, three hundred biscuits and a pipe of Malaga wine. An awning over the basin protected it from rain, which might have disturbed the chemical composition of the delicious beverage; and, in a charming little rose-wood boat, a cabin boy, belonging to the fleet, rowed about on the surface of the punch, ready to serve the joyous company, which numbered more than six thousand persons.*

## PARMIGIANO REGGIANO TERMINOLOGY

Parmigiano Reggiano, probably the finest Parmesan cheese, is made from unpasteurised skimmed cows' milk. A number of traditional terms are employed to indicate the time of year when the cheese was manufactured:

| term | months | | |
|------|--------|---|---|
| *maggengo* | April–November | *di tessa* | April–June |
| *invernengo* | December–March | *di centro* | July–August |
| | | *tardno* | September–November |

Other terms show the number of months the cheese has been matured:

*Nuovo* <17 months · *Vecchio* 18–24 months · *Stravecchio* >24 months

The term *ungia* (nail) is used to indicate the thickness of the cheese's rind.

## COFFEE CANTATA

J.S. Bach's Cantata (BWV 211), composed *c.*1732, is a comic opera based upon a libretto by the poet, Ober-Post-Commissarius, and tax-collector, Picander. The cantata has two nicknames, the first of which '*Schweigt stille, plaudert nicht*' derives from the opening lines of German ('Be silent, do not chatter'). The second nickname is the 'Coffee Cantata' which refers to the contemporary craze for coffee at which the opera pokes fun.

## SOME QUOTATIONS ON SMOKING

QUEEN ELIZABETH I · [to Sir Walter Raleigh] I have known many persons who turned their gold into smoke, but you are the first to turn smoke into gold.

RUDYARD KIPLING · … a woman is only a woman, but a good cigar is a Smoke.

COLETTE · When a wife can purchase her husband the right cigars, their relationship is blessed.

SHERLOCK HOLMES · It is quite a three-pipe problem…

MOLIÈRE · He who lives without tobacco is not worthy to live.

ROBERT BENCHLEY · Knocking out of a pipe can be made almost as important as the smoking of it, especially if there are nervous people in the room. A good, smart knock of a pipe against a tin wastebasket and you will have a neurasthenic out of his chair and into the window sash in no time.

WINSTON CHURCHILL · I always carry Cuba in my mouth.

JEAN SYLVAIN BAILLY · [on the eve of his execution] It's time for me to enjoy another pinch of snuff. Tomorrow my hands will be bound, so as to make it impossible.

SIR ARTHUR HELPS · What a blessing this smoking is! Perhaps the greatest that we owe to the discovery of America.

MARK TWAIN · To cease smoking is the easiest thing I ever did. I ought to know because I've done it a thousand times.

SIGMUND FREUD · I owe to the cigar a great intensification of my capacity to work and a facilitation of my self-control.

CLEMENT FREUD · If you resolve to give up smoking, drinking and loving, you don't actually live longer; it just seems longer.

CHE GUEVARA · An habitual and extremely important complement in the life of a guerrilla is smoking … for the smoke that he can expel in moments of relaxation is a great companion to the lonely soldier.

MOHAMMED DAUD KHAN ·
[President of Afghanistan 1973–78]
I feel the happiest when I can light my American cigarettes with Soviet matches.

DUC DE LA ROCHEFOUCAULD · The cigar is a great resource … it raises your spirits. Are you troubled by something? The cigar will dissolve it.

EDWARD BULWER-LYTTON · A good cigar is as great a comfort to a man as a good cry to a woman.

OSCAR WILDE · A cigarette is the perfect type of a perfect pleasure. It is exquisite, and it leaves one unsatisfied. What more can one want?     [*The Picture of Dorian Grey*]

## PRICES UNDER EDWARD I

In *c.*1272, the Mayor of London, responding to public concern over the price of food, set a fixed tariff for provisions. Some of those prices were:

| | | | |
|---|---|---|---|
| Best hen......... | three half-pence | Pheasant .............. | four pence |
| Pullet............ | three half-pence | Heron ................... | six pence |
| Capon................. | two pence | Swan............... | three shillings |
| Goose................... | five pence | Crane.............. | three shillings |
| Wild goose............ | four pence | Best peacock ........... | one penny |
| Pigeons, three for ...... | one penny | Best coney ............. | four pence |
| Mallard, three for.... | a half-penny | Best hare .. three pence half-penny | |
| Plover.................. | one penny | Best lamb *(Christmas-Lent)* . | six pence |
| Partridge ......... | three half-pence | Best lamb *(other times)* ... | four pence |

## CHINESE RESTAURANT SYNDROME & MSG

Chinese Restaurant Syndrome is a collection of symptoms – ranging from flushes, headache, and swelling, to numbness, palpitations, and chest pain – which can present shortly after eating Chinese food. The syndrome was first described by R.H.M. Kwok (*N. Engl. J. Med.* 1968;278:796). In almost all cases the symptoms are mild and tend to fade within a few hours. The cause of the syndrome remains uncertain, and although anecdotal evidence has always suggested a link with the flavour enhancer monosodium glutamate (MSG), a number of recent randomised, double-blind trials have cast doubt over such assertions. The US Food and Drug Administration has stated that MSG 'is a safe food ingredient for the general population' classifying it GRAS – 'Generally Recognized As Safe'.

## A FEW MEXICAN TORTILLA DISHES

*Tortillas* – round flatbreads made from corn or flour – are a staple element of Mexican cuisine and form the basis of a many classic dishes:

Burritos....................................*soft tortillas, filled and rolled up*
Enchiladas ...........*filled tortillas, rolled, covered with a sauce and baked*
Tostadas .................*flat tortillas, fried and topped with various things*
Nachos ...................*fried tortilla chips, grilled with cheese and chillis*
Quesadillas.........................*folded tortilla 'sandwiches' with cheese*
Tacos......................................*corn tortillas folded and filled*
Totopos...............................*slices of tortilla deep-fried until crisp*
Chilaquiles .......*crisp tortillas topped with, cheese, chilli, salsa, onion, etc.*
Chimichangas ....*fried tortilla parcels filled with onion, cheese, potato, etc.*

## —— CONTRACTUAL FOOD & DRINK DEMANDS ——

Musicians' contracts often carry highly detailed clauses (riders) specifying the arrangements they require backstage – below are a few brief extracts:

| | |
|---|---|
| Cher | *2 20oz bottles of Cherry Rush Gatorade* |
| Frank Sinatra | *24 chilled jumbo shrimp* |
| Snoop Dogg | *'fried foods are a tour staple'* |
| Prince | *herbal teas, honey, four lemons* |
| Guns N' Roses | *1 order of fettucini Alfredo* |
| Britney Spears | *1 bag Cool Ranch Doritos; 1 box Altoids red* |
| Tina Turner | *1 pint chocolate milk* |
| Elton John | *'absolutely no cold cuts'* |
| Kiss | *6 caramel rice cakes* |
| Burt Bacharach | *creamy peanut butter* |
| The Beach Boys | *one small bowl white (no red) pistachio nuts* |
| ZZ Top | *1 can squeeze American cheese* |
| Barenaked Ladies | *large assorted fruit plate for 12 (be creative please...)* |
| Rolling Stones | *'smart, well groomed hostesses to assist in serving food'* |
| Aerosmith | *corn on the cob; fresh ears, cooked 3 minutes only* |
| The Who | *small vegetable tray; deli tray; large fruit bowl* |
| Lynyrd Skynyrd | *fresh fruit in season, with plenty of watermelon* |

## —— EATING SWANS ——

Swans are not, as popularly thought, royal birds (in the sense that the sturgeon is a royal fish) although the Crown has asserted prerogative rights over swans since the C12th. In 1483 legislation restricted ownership of swans to those with a property freehold greater than five shillings. In 1496 the stealing of swans' eggs was punishable by a year in prison. Over the centuries the Crown has issued a number of licences to keep and eat swans – notably to two Worshipful Companies, Vintners and Dyers, and to other fitting institutions. The Feast Book of St John's College, Cambridge, records swans as being eaten at Christmas (1879–1894) in such dishes as swans' giblet soup. Nowadays the Crown's right over swans is enshrined in the *Wild Creatures & Forest Laws Act* (1971); and the consumption of swans is prohibited by the *Wildlife & Countryside Act* (1981).

The following is a C15th recipe for preparing roast swan:
*Kutte* [cut] *a Swan in the rove* [roof] *of the mouthe toward the brayne enlonge, and lete him blede, and kepe the blode for chawdewyn* [entrails]*; or else knytte a knot on his nek, and so late his nekke breke; then skald him. Draw him and roast him even as thou doest goce* [geese] *in all poyntes, and serve him forth with chawdewyn.*

# —— QUICK REFERENCE WINE VINTAGE GUIDE ——

| | 2000 | 1999 | 1998 | 1997 | 1996 | 1995 | 1994 | 1990 | 1989 | 1988 | 1986 | 1985 | 1983 | 1982 |
|---|---|---|---|---|---|---|---|---|---|---|---|---|---|---|
| FRANCE · ALSACE | ⊕ | O | ⊕ | O | ☆ | ☆ | O | ☆ | ☆ | ☆ | O | ☆ | ☆ | |
| BORDEAUX [red] · Médoc/Graves | ⊕ | ⊕ | ⊕ | O | ⊕ | ⊕ | O | ☆ | ☆ | ☆ | O | O | O | ☆ |
| St-Emilion/Pomerol | ⊕ | ⊕ | ⊕ | O | O | O | ☆ | O | ☆ | ☆ | O | ☆ | O | ☆ |
| BORDEAUX [white] · Graves | O | O | O | O | O | O | | ☆ | ☆ | ☆ | O | O | O | O |
| Sauternes/Barsac | ⊕ | ⊕ | ⊕ | ⊕ | ⊕ | ⊕ | | ☆ | ☆ | ☆ | O | ☆ | ☆ | |
| BURGUNDY [red] · Côte de Beune | ⊕ | ⊕ | ⊕ | O | ⊕ | ☆ | O | ☆ | ☆ | O | O | O | | |
| Beaujolais/Mâcon | O | O | O | O | O | ☆ | | | | | | | | |
| BURGUNDY [white] · Chablis | O | O | O | O | O | O | | ☆ | ☆ | O | | O | | |
| Côte de Beune | ⊕ | ⊕ | O | O | ⊕ | ☆ | | ☆ | ☆ | O | | ☆ | | |
| Mâconnaise/Chalonnaise | O | O | | | O | ☆ | | ☆ | ☆ | O | | O | | |
| RHÔNE [red] · Hermitage | ⊕ | ⊕ | ⊕ | O | ⊕ | ☆ | O | ☆ | ☆ | ☆ | O | ☆ | ☆ | ☆ |
| Châteauneuf-du-Pape | ⊕ | ⊕ | ⊕ | ☆ | O | ☆ | O | ☆ | ☆ | ☆ | O | ☆ | ☆ | ☆ |
| RHÔNE [white] | ⊕ | ⊕ | ⊕ | O | O | ☆ | O | ☆ | ☆ | O | O | O | O | |
| LOIRE | O | O | O | ☆ | O | | | ☆ | ☆ | O | O | O | | |
| CHAMPAGNE | ⊕ | ⊕ | | ☆ | ☆ | | ☆ | ☆ | ☆ | ☆ | O | O | | |
| NEW ZEALAND [red] | O | O | ☆ | O | ☆ | ☆ | O | O | O | | | | | |
| AUSTRALIA [red] · New Sth Wales | ⊕ | ☆ | ☆ | | | O | | ☆ | ☆ | ☆ | | O | | |
| South Australia | ⊕ | ⊕ | ⊕ | ⊕ | ☆ | | ☆ | O | ☆ | ☆ | O | | | ☆ |
| Victoria | ⊕ | ☆ | ☆ | O | ☆ | | O | ☆ | | O | ☆ | | | ☆ |
| Tasmania | ⊕ | ⊕ | ⊕ | ☆ | O | ☆ | ☆ | O | ☆ | ☆ | ☆ | O | O | |
| Western Australia | ⊕ | ⊕ | ☆ | ☆ | ☆ | ☆ | ☆ | O | ☆ | ☆ | ☆ | O | O | |
| ITALY [red] · Barolo/Barbaresco | ⊕ | ⊕ | ⊕ | O | ⊕ | O | | ☆ | ☆ | O | | O | O | |
| Tuscany | ⊕ | ⊕ | O | O | O | O | | ☆ | ☆ | O | O | O | O | |
| Veneto | ⊕ | ☆ | O | ☆ | O | O | | ☆ | | ☆ | | ☆ | | |
| The South & Islands | O | ☆ | O | O | | | | | | | | | | |
| SPAIN [red] · Rioja | ⊕ | ⊕ | O | | ☆ | ☆ | ☆ | ☆ | ☆ | O | | O | ☆ | |
| Ribera del Duero | | ⊕ | | ☆ | O | O | ☆ | ☆ | | O | | | O | |
| USA · CALIFORNIA · White | ☆ | ☆ | ☆ | O | ☆ | ☆ | ☆ | ☆ | O | | ☆ | | | |
| [red] North of San Francisco | ⊕ | ⊕ | | ⊕ | ☆ | ☆ | ☆ | ☆ | | | O | ☆ | | |
| [red] South of San Francisco | | ⊕ | O | O | ☆ | ☆ | O | O | | | ☆ | | | |
| GERMANY · Rhine | O | O | | O | O | ☆ | | ☆ | O | O | | | O | |
| Mosel | O | ☆ | | O | O | ☆ | | ☆ | O | O | | | O | |
| SOUTH AMERICA · [red] | | ☆ | ☆ | ☆ | | ☆ | O | ☆ | | | | | | |
| SOUTH AFRICA · [red] | ☆ | O | ☆ | O | | ☆ | O | | O | | O | ☆ | | |

| | 2000 | 1997 | 1994 | 1992 | 1991 | 1985 | 1983 | 1980 | 1977 | 1970 | 1966 | 1963 | 1955 | 1948 |
|---|---|---|---|---|---|---|---|---|---|---|---|---|---|---|
| VINTAGE PORT | ⊕ | ⊕ | ⊕ | ⊕ | ⊕ | ☆ | O | ☆ | ☆ | ☆ | ☆ | ☆ | ☆ | ☆ |

*This is a very elementary guide to some of the most drinkable wines from a few 'classic' regions.*
*⊕ = wine for laying down · O = good wine to drink now · ☆ = excellent wine to drink now*

## C18TH SCOTTISH BREAKFAST

The breakfast at the house of Maclean of Torloisk, Isle of Mull, *c.*1784

Porridge with Cream · Salted Herrings · Eggs · Smoked Beef-ham
Flummery of Milk, Eggs, Sugar, and Rum
Butter · Cheese · Barley Cakes · Oatcakes · Sea Biscuit
Currant Jelly · Blaeberry Jam · Jamaica Rum

## ALCOHOLICS ANONYMOUS 12 STEPS

Founded in America shortly after the repeal of Prohibition in 1935, Alcoholics Anonymous is now a worldwide organisation dedicated to assisting its members overcome alcoholism and maintain sobriety. At the heart of AA is a set of informal, voluntary guides known as the '12 Steps':

1. *We admitted we were powerless over alcohol – that our lives had become unmanageable.* 2. *Came to believe that a Power greater than ourselves could restore us to sanity.* 3. *Made a decision to turn our will and our lives over to the care of God as we understood Him.* 4. *Made a searching and fearless moral inventory of ourselves.* 5. *Admitted to God, to ourselves and to another human being the exact nature of our wrongs.* 6. *Were entirely ready to have God remove all these defects of character.* 7. *Humbly asked Him to remove our short-comings.* 8. *Made a list of all persons we had harmed, and became willing to make amends to them all.* 9. *Made direct amends to such people wherever possible, except when to do so would injure them or others.* 10. *Continued to take personal inventory and when we were wrong promptly admitted it.* 11. *Sought through prayer and meditation to improve our conscious contact with God, as we understood Him, praying only for knowledge of His will for us and the power to carry that out.* 12. *Having had a spiritual awakening as the result of these steps, we tried to carry this message to alcoholics, and to practice these principles in all our affairs.*

## SOME FOOD AS SLANG AND INSULT

| Food term | derogatory term for |
|---|---|
| Bean-eater | Latin-Americans |
| Cheese-eater | Dutchmen |
| Chicken | cowards |
| Chilli-eater | Mexicans |
| Fish-eater | Catholics |
| Frog | French |
| Garlic-eater | French; Yugoslavians |
| Goulash | Hungarians |
| Ham | second-rate over-actor |
| Herring-snapper | Scandinavians |
| Kraut | Germans |
| Limey | English |
| Macaroni | Italians (See p.13.) |
| Pom(egranate?) | English |
| Rosbifs, les | English |

## MICHELIN STARS

The *Michelin Guide* was first published in 1900 by the Michelin Tyre Company – founded two years earlier by brothers André and Édouard Michelin. Since then the Guide has become famed for its selection of the very best restaurants. A three-star rating system is employed on a deceptively simple set of criteria: [*] 'A very good restaurant in its category'; [**] 'Excellent cooking, worth a detour'; [***] 'Exceptional cuisine, worth a special trip'. In reality, the award of just one Michelin star confers instant recognition on both restaurant and chef, two stars confers fame, and a three-star rating is the culinary equivalent of a Nobel prize. At the time of writing, only 12 British restaurants have two or three stars:

| HEAD CHEF | RESTAURANT | LOCATION |
| --- | --- | --- |
| Michel Roux | *Waterside Inn* *** | Bray-on-Thames |
| Gordon Ramsay | *Gordon Ramsay* *** | London |
| Heston Blumenthal | *Fat Duck* ** | Bray-on-Thames |
| Michael Caines | *Gidleigh Park* ** | Chagford |
| David Everitt-Matthias | *Le Champignon Sauvage* ** | Cheltenham |
| Eric Chavot | *Capital* ** | London |
| Michel Roux, Jr | *Le Gavroche* ** | London |
| John Burton-Race | *John Burton-Race* ** | London |
| Shane Osborn | *Pied à Terre* ** | London |
| Philip Howard | *The Square* ** | London |
| Raymond Blanc | *Le Manoir aux Quat' Saisons* ** | Oxford |
| Germain Schwab | *Winteringham Fields* ** | Winteringham |

## EDWARD LEAR'S NONSENSE COOKERY

### To make Gosky Patties

Take a Pig, 3 or 4 years of age, and tie him by the off hind leg to a post. Place 5 pounds of currants, 3 of sugar, 2 pecks of peas, 18 roast chestnuts, a candle and 6 bushels of turnips within his reach; if he eats these, constantly provide him with more. Then, procure some cream, some slices of Cheshire cheese, four quires of foolscap paper and a packet of black pins. Work the whole into a paste, and spread it out to dry on a sheet of clean brown waterproof linen. When the paste is perfectly dry, but not before, proceed to beat the Pig violently, with the handle of a large broom. If he squeals, beat him again. Visit the paste and beat the pig alternately for some days, and ascertain that if at the end of that period the whole is about to turn into *Gosky Patties*. If it does not then, it never will; and in that case the Pig may be let loose, and the whole process may be considered as finished.

## THE BOLOGNESE SCHOOL

The Bolognese School of painting was influential in developing the Roman baroque style, and it had three distinctive periods: the *Early*, founded by Zoppo (C15th); the *Roman* by Bagnacavallo (C16th); and the *Eclectic* by Carracci (late C16th). It seems that, throughout its history, the Bolognese School has enjoyed no association whatsoever with spaghetti.

## FOOD SAFETY COLOUR CODES

In order to comply with food safety standards many kitchens and catering establishments colour-code their knives, chopping boards, and storage equipment to avoid cross-contamination. One colour-coding system is:

| | | | | |
|---|---|---|---|---|
| WHITE | bakery & dairy | | YELLOW | cooked meat |
| GREEN | salad & fruit | | BROWN | vegetables |
| RED | raw meat | | BLUE | raw fish |

Colour-coded labels are used to ensure food is not kept after a certain day:

| | | | | |
|---|---|---|---|---|
| BLUE | Monday | | GREEN | Friday |
| YELLOW | Tuesday | | ORANGE | Saturday |
| RED | Wednesday | | BLACK | Sunday |
| BROWN | Thursday | | *(Other colour-coding conventions exist.)* | |

## FOIE GRAS

Considered by some to be unspeakably (and uneatably) cruel, *foie gras* is the liver of a goose or duck which has been grossly enlarged by force-feeding. (According to *Larousse,* the record goose liver weight is 2kg.) Most accounts trace *foie gras* back to Roman times, when geese were crammed with figs. Cato, Columella, and Palladius all give instructions for making the delicacy; indeed, Emperor Heliogabalus – noted for his brief reign (AD218–222) of debauched excess and homosexual orgies – fed *foie gras* to his dogs. However, it is claimed that *foie gras* was known in Egyptian times, based upon illustrations of force-feeding found inside the tomb of the celebrated Fifth Dynasty official Ti (*fl.*2430BC). The ideal accompaniment to *foie gras* is usually considered to be Sauterne or sherry, though there are some who advocate port, Madeira, or even Champagne. Grimod de la Reynière drank Swiss absinthe with *foie gras,* but warned:

> …nothing surpasses an excellent *pâté de foie gras*:
> they have killed more gourmands than the plague.

## FLETCHERISM

Fletcherism was a nutritional system – and philosophy of life – devised by Horace Fletcher MA (1849–1919) after he was refused life-insurance for being too fat. Fletcher's system sought to regulate the appetite and the mechanics of eating to create a healthy body and a sound mind: '…the Crux of Fletcherism is found in first training the muscular and mental apparatus to proceed with thorough deliberation relative to everything taken into the body, for from this intake … comes efficiency or inefficiency.' Curiously, Fletcherism was influenced by the British Prime Minister William Gladstone, who is reported to have advised children:

> *Chew your food thirty-two times at least, so as to give*
> *each of your thirty-two teeth a chance at it.*

At the time Fletcherism was parodied as the 'chew-chew cult' and many mocked Fletcher for advocating nothing more than 'excessive mastication'. Yet Fletcherism did have a number of notable advocates, including John D. Rockefeller, who claimed the system was a means of 'slaughtering' the 'demon indigestion'. Fletcherism's Five Principles were:

1. Wait for a true, earned appetite.
2. Select from the food available that which appeals most to appetite, and in the order called for by appetite.
3. Get all the good taste there is in food out of it in the mouth, and swallow only when it practically 'swallows itself'.
4. Enjoy the good taste for all it is worth, and do not allow any depressing or diverting thought to intrude upon the ceremony.
5. Wait; take and *enjoy as much as possible* what appetite approves; Nature will do the rest.

The publishers of *Fletcherism – what it is; or How I Became Young at Sixty* (1913) claimed in a somewhat bold foreword: 'It is safe to say that no intelligent reader will peruse this work without becoming convinced that Mr Fletcher's principles as to eating and living are the sanest that have ever been propounded.'

## COOKERY vs. ASTRONOMY

> *I regard the discovery of a new dish as far more interesting an event than the discovery of a star, for we have always stars enough. I shall not regard the sciences as sufficiently honoured nor appropriately represented among us, so long as I do not see a cook in the first class of the Institute.*

Thus spake the physician M. Henrion de Pensey (President of the Court of Cassation) to the astronomer Pierre Simon de Laplace (*c.*1810).

# —A FEW RECOMMENDED ESTABLISHMENTS—

| HOME | ABROAD |
|---|---|
| *Odettes* . . . . . . . . . . . . . . . . . London NW1 | *Els Tinars* . . . . . . . Sant Féliu, Girona, Spain |
| *Mirabelle* . . . . . . . . . . . . . . . . . London W1 | *Impression* . . . . . . . . . . . . . Berlin, Germany |
| *Andrew Edmunds* . . . . . . . . London W1 | *Caffe Reggio* . . . . . . . . . . . New York, USA |
| *Rules* . . . . . . . . . . . . . . . . . . London WC2E | *Au Bistro de la Sorbonne*. . . Paris, France |
| *The Abingdon* . . . . . . . . . . . . London W8 | *Da Fiore* . . . . . . . . . . . . . . . . . Venice, Italy |
| *Browns Hotel* . . . . . . . . . . . . . . . . London | *Mustards Grill* . . . . . . . . . . . . Napa, USA |
| *Capriccio* . . . . . . . . . . . . . . . London NW11 | *Three Brothers Inn* . . . . . . . Bali, Indonesia |
| *The Ivy* . . . . . . . . . . . . . . . . . . . London W1 | *Ocean Sports Hotel* . . . . . Watamu, Kenya |
| *The Fleet Tandoori* . . . . . . . London NW3 | *Au Bon Saint-Pourcain* . . . . Paris, France |
| *The Tickell Arms*. Whittlesford, Cambridge | *Banana Leaf Apolo* . . . . . . . . . . Singapore |
| *The Savoy Grill* . . . . . . . . . . . London W1 | *The Bounty Hotel* . . . . . . . Bali, Indonesia |
| *Stac Polly* . . . . . . . . . . . . . . . . . . Edinburgh | *Al Cavallino Bianco* . . . . . . . . Rome, Italy |
| *The Parsee* . . . . . . . . . . . . . London, N19 | *La Gare* . . . . . . . . . . . . . . . . Paris, France |
| *The Green Dragon* . Stoke Fleming, Devon | *Can Ganassa* . . . . . . . . . . Barcelona, Spain |
| *Kebabish Original* . . Stanmore, Middlesex | *Doyle's* . . . . . . . . . . . . . . Sydney, Australia |
| *Wiltons* . . . . . . . . . . . . . . . . . London SW1 | *Corte Sconta* . . . . . . . . . . . . . Venice, Italy |
| *Tir-a-Môr* . . . . . . . . . . Criccieth, N. Wales | *Tribeca Grill* . . . . . . . . . . . New York, USA |
| *Gidleigh Park Hotel* . . . . Chagford, Devon | *Villa Santi* . . . . . . . . . . Luang Prabang, Laos |
| *Square & Compass Inn* . . . . . . . . Dorset | *Enoteca Pinchiorri* . . . . . . . Florence, Italy |
| *Porthminster Beach Café* . . . . . Cornwall | *L'Astrance* . . . . . . . . . . . . . . . Paris, France |
| *Green Cottage* . . . . . . . . . . . London NW3 | *Fog City Diner* . . . . . . . San Francisco, USA |
| *Sankey's Wine Bar*. . Tunbridge Wells, Kent | *Boboli Gardens Café* . . . . . . Florence, Italy |
| *Bar Italia* . . . . . . . . . . . . . . . . London W1 | *Spec's* . . . . . . . . . . . . . San Francisco, USA |
| *Le Gavroche* . . . . . . . . . . . . . . London W1 | *Es Moli de Foc* . . . . . . . . . . Menorca, Spain |
| *The Wolseley* . . . . . . . . . . . . . London W1 | *L'Ulmet* . . . . . . . . . . . . . . . . . . Milan, Italy |
| *Louis Tea Rooms* . . . . . . . . London NW3 | *Weber's* . . . . . . . . . . . . . . . Ontario, Canada |
| *The Green* . . . . . . . . . . . . . London SE22 | *Woody Creek Tavern* . . . . . . . Aspen, USA |
| *La Gaffe (café)* . . . . . . . . . . London NW3 | *La Grange* . . . . . . . . Les Contamines, France |
| *The Ship Inn* . . . . . . . . Itchenor, Chichester | *Tortilla Flats* . . . . . . . . . . New York, USA |
| *Le Manoir aux Quat' Saisons* . . Oxford | *Scaramouche* . . . . . . . . . . . Toronto, Canada |
| *Vertigo 42* . . . . . . . . . . . . . London, EC2 | *Gyoza Centre* . . . . . . . . . . . . Hakone, Japan |
| *St John* . . . . . . . . . . . . . . . . . London EC1 | *Ristorante Belvedere* . . . . . . La Morra, Italy |
| *22 Chesterton Road* . . . . . . . . Cambridge | *Antica Osteria da Divo* . . . . . Siena, Italy |
| *Coombe House Hotel* . . Gittisham, Devon | *Aries* . . . . . . . . . Little Corn Island, Nicaragua |
| *Taro* . . . . . . . . . . . . . . . . . . . London NW3 | *i Truli* . . . . . . . . . . . . . . . . New York, USA |
| *La Trouvaille* . . . . . . . . . . . . . London W1 | *The Stokehouse* . . . . . . Melbourne, Australia |
| *Le Caprice* . . . . . . . . . . . . . London SW1 | *Yacout* . . . . . . . . . . . . . Marrakesh Morocco |
| *Port-na-Craig Inn* . . . . . . . . . . . Pitlochry | *Le Louis XV* . . . . . . Monte Carlo, Monaco |
| *Lee Ho Fook* . . . . . . . . . . . . . London W1 | *Le Rubis* . . . . . . . . . . . . . . . . Paris, France |
| *Chez Bruce* . . . . . . . . . . . . London SW17 | *The Tavern on Rush* . . . . . . Chicago, USA |
| *Cecconi's* . . . . . . . . . . . . . . . . London W1 | *Mudbrick Vinyeard* . . . . . Waiheke I., NZ |
| *The Merchant House* . . . . . . . . . Ludlow | *L'Atelier de Joel Robuchon*. . Paris, France |

## —SOME FURTHER READING—

*De re coquinaria libri decem*............?Marcus Gavius Apicius, *c*.AD30?
*The Forme of Cury*........'the Master-Cooks of King Richard II', *c*.1390
*The Booke of Kervinge*................Wynkyn de Worde (printer), 1508
*Opera divisa in sei libri*........................Bartolomeo Scappi, 1570
*The Accomplisht Cook*..........................Robert May, 1685
*Le Traité des Ailments*....................Louis Lemery, 1702
*Some Observations on the Irritability of Vegetables*........J.E. Smith, 1788
*Almanach des Gourmands*..................Grimod de la Reynière, 1803
*Le Mâitre d'hôtel Français*.......................Antonin Carême, 1822
*La Physiologie du goût*..............Jean-Anthelme Brillat-Savarin, 1826
*Modern Cookery for Private Families*...................Eliza Acton, 1845
*The Pantropheon*...........................................Alexis Soyer, 1853
*The Curiosities of Food*......................Peter Lund Simmonds, 1859
*Beeton's Book of Household Management*............Isabella Beeton, 1861
*Le Grand Dictionnaire de cuisine*.................Alexandre Dumas, 1873
*Gigantic Cuttle-fish*.........................William Saville Kent, 1879
*On Leprosy and Fish Eating*..............Sir Jonathan Hutchinson, 1906
*Indian Fish of Proved Utility as Mosquito-Destroyers*.......S. Sewell, 1912
*Potatoes as Food and Medicine*............Henry Valentine Knaggs, 1930
*The Savoy Cocktail Book*...........................Harry Craddock, 1933
*The True Drunkard's Delight*......................William Juniper, 1933
*The Art of Faking Exhibition Poultry*...........George Ryley Scott, 1934
*The Toothbrush: Its Use and Abuse*.................Isador Hirschfeld, 1939
*Historic Tinned Foods*....................Sir Jack Cecil Drummond, 1939
*The Gastronomical Me*...............................M.F.K. Fisher, 1943
*Venus in the Kitchen*............................Norman Douglas, 1952
*Be Bold With Bananas*........South Africa Banana Control Board, 1970
*Why Popeye Took Spinach*.....R. Hunter, *The Lancet*, i;(7702):746–7, 1971
*Note on the Burundi Food Industry*.....Dept. of Trade & Industry, 1989
*Rancidity in Foods*..............J.C. Allen & R.J. Hamilton (eds.), 1994
*Savoury Flavours*...........................Tilak W. Nagodawithana, 1995
*Real Good Food*...................................Nigel Slater, 1995
*Bad Breath: a Multidisciplinary Approach*.....D. van Steenberghe, 1996
*A Complete Course on Canning* (13th edn.)...........D.L. Downing, 1996
*The Debt to Pleasure*..........................John Lanchester, 1996
*The Book of Jewish Food*...........................Claudia Roden, 1997
*Proceedings of the 5th Cheese Symposium*......Tim M. Cogan (ed.), 1997
*Practical Dehydration*........................Maurice Greensmith, 1998
*Bubbles in Food*............................Grant M. Campbell (ed.), 1999
*Spam – The Cookbook*.........................Marguerite Patten, 2000
*Technology of Biscuits, Crackers, & Cookies*........Duncan Manley, 2000
*The Wilder Shores of Gastronomy*..............Alan Davidson (ed.), 2002
*Feast: a History of Grand Eating*....................Sir Roy Strong, 2002

Bad indexers are everywhere, and what is most singular is that each one makes the same sort of blunders – blunders which it would seem impossible that anyone could make, until we find these same blunders over and over again in black and white.

— HENRY B. WHEATLEY, *How to Make an Index,* 1902

––––––– ABSINTHE – CAFFEINATED DRINKS –––––––

─────── SLANG AND INSULT – ZOO, EATING ───────

The cook was a good cook, as cooks go;
and as cooks go, she went.

— SAKI · *Hector Hugh Munro* (1870–1916)

──────── MISCELLANEOUS OCCURRENCES────────

| Item | No. of mentions |
| --- | --- |
| Chocolate | 35 |
| Ortolan | 17 |
| Eggs | 84 |
| Chickens | 36 |
| Ptarmigan | 1 |
| Salads | 32 |
| Tea | 34 |
| Coffee | 29 |
| Fugu | 28 |
| Milk | 44 |
| Cheese | 54 |
| Cakes | 13 |
| Bread | 56 |
| Wine | 70 |
| Water | 37 |
| Lemons | 20 |
| Butter | 20 |
| Asparagus | 14 |
| Fish | 20 |
| Chips | 5 |
| Horses | 10 |
| Word count | 48,380 |

*– finis –*